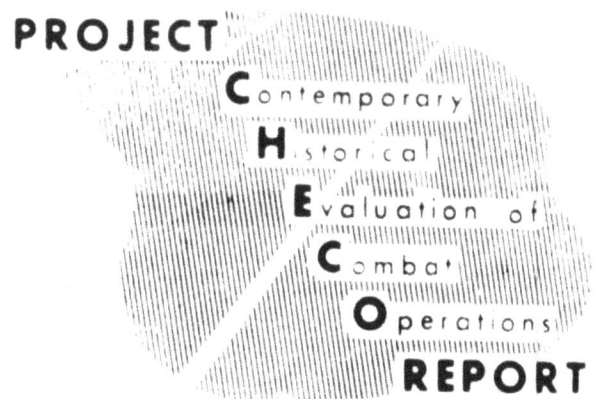

PROJECT
Contemporary
Historical
Evaluation of
Combat
Operations
REPORT

THE WAR IN VIETNAM
JULY-DECEMBER 1967

29 NOVEMBER 1968

HQ PACAF
Directorate, Tactical Evaluation
CHECO Division

Prepared by:
LEE BONETTI
MAJOR A. W. THOMPSON
MELVIN F PORTER
C. WILLIAM THORNDALE
Project CHECO 7th AF, DOAC

REPLY TO
ATTN OF: DOTEC

29 November 1968

SUBJECT: Project CHECO Report, "The War in Vietnam, July-December 1967" (U)

TO: SEE DISTRIBUTION PAGE

1. Attached is a SECRET NOFORN document. It shall be transported, stored, safeguarded, and accounted for in accordance with applicable security directives. Each page is marked according to its contents. SPECIAL HANDLING REQUIRED, NOT RELEASABLE TO FOREIGN NATIONALS. The information contained in this document will not be disclosed to foreign nationals or their representatives. Retain or destroy in accordance with AFR 205-1. Do not return.

2. This letter does not contain classified information and may be declassified if attachment is removed from it.

FOR THE COMMANDER IN CHIEF

WARREN H. PETERSON, Colonel, USAF
Chief, CHECO Division
Directorate, Tactical Evaluation
DCS/Operations

1 Atch
Proj CHECO Rpt (SNF),
29 Nov 68

DISTRIBUTION

HQ USAF		MAJCOM		PACAF	
AFAAC	1 Cy	SAFOI	2 Cys	19AF (DA-C)	1 Cy
AFAMA	1 Cy	SAFLL	1 Cy	USAFAGOS	1 Cy
AFBSA	1 Cy	SAFAA	1 Cy	USAFSAWC (DO)	1 Cy
AFCCS-SA	1 Cy			USAFTAWC (DA)	1 Cy
AFCHO	2 Cys	**MAJCOM**		USAFTARC (DI)	1 Cy
AFGOA	2 Cys	AU (ASI-HA)	2 Cys	USAFTALC (DA)	1 Cy
AFIIN	1 Cy	AU (ASI-ASAD)	1 Cy	USAFTFWC (CRCD)	1 Cy
AFISI	3 Cys	AU (AUL3T-66-7)	1 Cy	FTD (TDPI)	1 Cy
AFISL	1 Cy	AU (ACSC)	1 Cy	AFAITC	1 Cy
AFMSG	1 Cy	ADC (ADODC)	1 Cy	SRAFREP (SWC)	1 Cy
AFNINA	1 Cy	ADC (ADOOP)	2 Cys		
AFNINCC	1 Cy	ADC (ADLPP)	2 Cys	**PACAF**	
AFNINDE	3 Cys	TAC (DO-O)	1 Cy	DP	1 Cy
AFOAPS	1 Cy	TAC (DPL)	2 Cys	DI	1 Cy
AFOCC	1 Cy	TAC (DOTS)	1 Cy	DO	1 Cy
AFOCE	1 Cy	TAC (DORQ)	1 Cy	DPL	1 Cy
AFOMO	1 Cy	TAC (DI)	1 Cy	DXIH	1 Cy
AFOWX	1 Cy	MAC (MAFOI)	1 Cy	5AF (DOP)	1 Cy
AFPDP	1 Cy	MAC (MAOID)	1 Cy	7AF (DOAC)	9 Cys
AFPMRE	1 Cy	MAC (MAOCO)	1 Cy	13AF (DOP)	1 Cy
AFRDC	1 Cy	AFSC (SCL)	8 Cys	13AF (DXI)	1 Cy
AFRDR	1 Cy	AFSC (SCO)	2 Cys	834AIRDIV	1 Cy
AFRDQ	1 Cy	AFLC (MCO)	1 Cy	3TFW	1 Cy
AFSLP	1 Cy	AFLC (MCF)	1 Cy	8TFW	1 Cy
AFSMS	1 Cy	ATC (ATXDC)	1 Cy	12TFW	1 Cy
AFSME	1 Cy	SAC (DO)	1 Cy	14SOW	1 Cy
AFSSS	1 Cy	SAC (DPL)	1 Cy	31TFW	1 Cy
AFSTP	1 Cy	SAC (DXI)	1 Cy	35TFW	1 Cy
AFXOP	1 Cy	SAC (DIX)	1 Cy	37TFW	1 Cy
AFXOPS	1 Cy	SAC (OA)	1 Cy	56SOW	1 Cy
AFXOSL	1 Cy	USAFA (DFH)	1 Cy	315SOW	1 Cy
AFXOSO	1 Cy	USAFE (OPL)	2 Cys	355TFW	1 Cy
AFXOSN	1 Cy	USAFSO (BIOH)	1 Cy	366TFW	1 Cy
AFXOPR	1 Cy	USAFSS (ODC)	1 Cy	388TFW	1 Cy
AFXOTZ	1 Cy	USAFSS (COI-5)	1 Cy	432TRW	1 Cy
AFXPD	9 Cys			460TRW (DCO)	1 Cy
AFXDOC	1 Cy	**OTHERS**		483TAW	1 Cy
AFXDOD	1 Cy	9AF (DO)	1 Cy	553RECON WG	1 Cy
AFXDOL	1 Cy	12AF (DI)	1 Cy	6400TEST SQ	1 Cy
				DOTEC	6 Cys

TABLE OF CONTENTS

	Page
FOREWORD	vii
CHAPTER I - ROLLING THUNDER	1
CHAPTER II - CLOSE AIR SUPPORT	18
COMBAT DRAGON	19
Loc Ninh	21
Dak To	24
Bo Duk	28
Enemy Counter-Air Tactics	28
CHAPTER III - TACTICAL AIR RECONNAISSANCE	31
Reconnaissance Force Structure	31
Changes in Operating Procedures over NVN	33
Reconnaissance Airframe Losses	35
Tactical Reconnaissance Sortie Accomplishment	36
CHAPTER IV - ARC LIGHT PROGRAM	39
Dak To	40
Operation NEUTRALIZE	41
Laos	44
Restrictions	44
Increased Sortie Effort	47
Bomb Damage Assessment	50
Interdiction	53
Psychological Effect	53
CHAPTER V - AIRLIFT	54
Organization	54
Redeployments	56
Tonnage	57
Tactical Airlift	58
Technology	59

	Page

CHAPTER VI - HERBICIDE OPERATIONS 62

        Reduced Sorties 62
        Revised Estimate 66
        Organization 66
        VNAF Participation 68
        DMZ Operations 70
        Effectiveness 71

CHAPTER VII - PSYCHOLOGICAL WARFARE 75

        Fact Sheet/Frantic Goat 75
        Increased Psyops Efforts 77
        New Developments 79
        Cambodian Border Test 82

CHAPTER VIII- BASE DEFENSE 84

        Da Nang 84
        Nha Trang 87
        Bien Hoa 88
        Tuy Hoa 89
        Base Defense Seminar 90

CHAPTER IX - NORTH VIETNAM AIR DEFENSE SYSTEM 96

        Antiaircraft Artillery 96
        Camouflage 101
        SAMs 102
        MIGs 106
        Degradation Plan 110

CHAPTER X - AIR FORCE ADVISORY GROUP 112

        Mission 112
        Organization 112
        Modernization 113
        Flying Safety 115
        Civic Action 116
        Evaluation 116

CHAPTER XI - SUMMARY OF MISSION AND RESOURCES 118

        Mission 118
        Resources 119
        Deployment 119
        Manning 120
        Aircraft Losses 122
        Munitions 123

Page

FOOTNOTES

Chapter I	125
Chapter II	127
Chapter III	128
Chapter IV	129
Chapter V	131
Chapter VI	132
Chapter VII	133
Chapter VIII	134
Chapter IX	136
Chapter X	138
Chapter XI	138

APPENDIXES

1.	USAF Combat Sorties - South Vietnam	140
2.	Total Munitions Delivered	141
3.	Destruction and Damage In-Country	142
4.	Completed Major U.S. Ground Operations	143
5.	USAF Aircraft Lost In-Country	144
6.	B-52 Sorties/Ordnance Expended	145

GLOSSARY 146

FIGURES   Follows Page

1.	Tactical Reconnaissance Assets - SEA	32
2.	Aircraft Loss Summary - 1 Jul-31 Dec 67	34
3.	Tactical Reconnaissance Programs - SEA	36
4.	Detailed Mosaic of Kep Airfield, NVN	38
5.	Thai Nguyen Thermal Power Plant	38
6.	Enemy AAA Emplacement	38
7.	Low Altitude Parachute Extraction System	60
8.	Eight Position AAA Battery	98
9.	USAF Aircraft Units in SVN	118

FOREWORD

"The War in Vietnam--July - December 1967" summarizes and provides an overall look at the Air Force role in North and South Vietnam for the semi-annual period. It is a continuation of the summary of Air Force operations first detailed in "The War in Vietnam - 1965".

ROLLING THUNDER gradually increased the weight of effort against a broadening, but still limited, target complex. The high incidence of radar-directed guns and SA-2s in the extended battle area also required changes in tactics by strike and reconnaissance forces. Close air support was instrumental in breaking the enemy attacks on Dak To, Loc Ninh, and Bo Duc, often by putting ordnance within 20 feet of prepared Allied positions. Airlift units retained their basic organizational structure and successfully supported the Allied requirements at Loc Ninh and Dak To. Flying safety was the paramount problem confronting the Vietnamese Air Force (VNAF), and by August, aircraft losses due to pilot error exceeded combat losses, until finally an intensive instrument training program was initiated. The denial of crops through herbicide destruction often placed a severe strain on the enemy supply system, forcing the North Vietnamese Army (NVA) out of their normal operating areas. Enemy attacks against air bases with a steadily improving rocket capability continued to present formidable problems. Successful efforts were made during the period to substantially increase the B-52 monthly sortie rate to keep pressure on the enemy's supply and infiltration system, while at the same time blocking his efforts to mass along the DMZ.

CHAPTER I

ROLLING THUNDER

The history of the ROLLING THUNDER campaign has been one of a slowly increasing weight of effort against a gradually broadening, but always carefully limited, range of military targets. Initially, a minimum weight of effort was employed against a small sector in the southern area of North Vietnam (NVN). When it became apparent that more pressure would be required, the operating area and level of effort were gradually increased, but sorties and targets remained under strict control.[1/]

During 1966, some important targets in the critical northeast area, such as petroleum and selected military facilities, were struck. However, the bulk of U.S. effort was directed against the southern Panhandle of North Vietnam in an effort to stem the flow of men and supplies into South Vietnam.[2/]

In early 1967, authorization was received to strike key targets including the electric power system, the steel industry, three airfields, and some high value components of the transportation system. By late May, these targets had all been struck and many of them heavily damaged. USAF operations during the latter half of 1967 were primarily a continuation of those initiated earlier in the year. North Vietnam's railroad system was the focal point of USAF efforts in Route Packages V and VIA. The destruction and disruption of key lines of communication (LOC), petroleum, oil, and lubricants (POL), and transportation targets in this area exceeded the results of any previous effort since the inception of the air campaign. Although railroads received the greatest effort, other significant targets included North Vietnam's jet-capable airfields and war-supporting industries. Air operations during the second half of the year were also characterized by the first U.S. engagement with Chinese Communist (CHICOM) MIGs over NVN, the first Air Force use of the Walleye glide bomb, a change in sortie allocations, an expanded target base, and the removal of restrictions against strikes within the Hanoi prohibited circle and in the CHICOM buffer zone. 3/

The basic objectives of the ROLLING THUNDER program remained unchanged: to reduce/restrict external assistance to North Vietnam; to destroy domestic war-supporting resources; to harass, disrupt, and impede the movement of men and material into South Vietnam and Laos. The campaign was never intended to completely stop infiltration, but it did reduce the level and thus adversely affected the enemy's capability to conduct major, sustained operations in South Vietnam. 4/

The growing weight of U.S. operations had also destroyed or disrupted half of North Vietnam's war-supporting resources. It had forced the enemy to disperse his petroleum in costly and inefficient small container storage systems. The bulk of the primary electric power capacity was destroyed. This, in turn, had adversely affected the chemical, rubber, and other power-dependent industries, and rendered inoperable the country's only iron and steel plant and its single cement plant. Many of the country's military complexes had been attacked. The interdiction of LOCs had significantly disrupted traffic and forced a major repair and reconstruction effort. Approximately 500,000 people were believed to have been diverted to reparation, reconstruction, and dispersion programs. The Hanoi regime faced mounting logistic, management, and morale problems. The northeast sector contained many fixed and transitory targets that had not been struck. Large quantities of supplies and war materiel from external sources were still moving into and through this area. These movements generated lucrative targets which required continued restrike to curtail their onward movement. 5/

USAF operations against North Vietnam continued to be conducted primarily from bases in Thailand. Udorn RTAFB had two squadrons of RF-4s and one squadron of F-4s; Ubon had four squadrons of F-4s; Korat had three squadrons of F-105s; U-Tapao had twenty-seven KC-135s; and Takhli had three squadrons of F-105s and eight KC-135s. A typical strike package consisted of F-105 and F-4 aircraft, Iron Hand, flak suppression, and MIG Combat Air Patrol aircraft. Iron Hand flights, normally composed of two F-105F Wild Weasel aircraft and two F-105D strike aircraft, led the strike package to the target area and were the best single counterforce against the SAM. The armament for the strike aircraft varied considerably based on the type of target. The most widely used weapons were the 500- and 750-pound bombs. The F-105 normally carried two 3,000-pound or six 750-pound bombs. The job of the flak suppression aircraft was to attack the AAA so that the strike aircraft could get through to the targets. The normal flak suppression weapons were CBUs and 3,000-pound bombs. The F-4 CAP aircraft, which carried air-to-air missiles, protected the strike package from MIGs. All aircraft making up the strike package carried radar jamming equipment in wing-mounted pods. These pods jammed enemy radar and in effect seriously degraded tracking of our aircraft for either AAA or SAM guidance. 6/

Other aircraft supporting the strike package included the Thailand-based KC-135s which were augmented, when required, by tankers based on Okinawa. Two refueling operations were required for strike aircraft--one on the way into North Vietnam and one on the return flight. EB-66 twin-engine jet aircraft preceded the strike package by approximately 30 minutes. Their mission was to locate enemy radar stations through triangulation and to jam the radar frequencies. The mission of the C-121 aircraft, COLLEGE EYE, was to monitor all air activity over North Vietnam and adjacent areas. Luzon was a C-135 aircraft which provided radio relay between strike and support aircraft and ground radio relay stations to the south. Depending upon the areas of operation and the MIG threat, these support aircraft might require F-4 fighter escort. Reconnaissance was an important facet of air operations and RF-4 aircraft out of Udorn conducted both pre-strike and post-strike missions.[7]

To facilitate strikes in North Vietnam, the country was divided into areas known as Route Packages. The 7AF was the coordinating authority for Route Package I, V, and VIA, while the Navy performed that function for the remaining packages--II, III, IV, and VIB. In July 1967, an agreement was reached between 7AF and CTF-77 for the purpose of establishing procedures by which cross operations between Air Force and Navy in RP I through IV and Laos could be more effectively managed and coordinated. CTF-77 and 7AF had, in being, systems that provided positive command and control of forces into and within their respective areas of responsibility. The basic goal of the July agreement was to permit utilization of 7AF strike diverts, on short notice, under CTF-77 coordination control in certain portions of Navy Route Packages when CTF-77 aircraft were not operating in those areas. It was hoped that this would increase the effectiveness of tactical airpower in North Vietnam and minimize mutual interference between 7AF and CTF-77 aircraft. These procedures would eliminate the requirement to designate sector assignments or point targets in the daily frag order which would specify Navy control for the second target with supplementary instruction as required.[8]

The focal point of the air campaign in the northern Route Packages was the interdiction of the railroad system north of Hanoi connecting North Vietnam with China that carried an estimated 70 percent of all North Vietnam's military supplies. During July, the weather was generally favorable and the Air Force had outstanding success in destroying or damaging boxcars, locomotives, and rail yards. The constant bombing of rail facilities forced the enemy to concentrate a massive construction and defense effort on keeping the rail lines partially serviceable.[9]

The CINCPAC allocation of 5,000 attack sorties to CINCPACFLT, 2,500 Thai-based attack sorties to COMUSMACV, and 2,600 to CINCPACAF for use in their respective areas of responsibility was cancelled in July. The commanders were "authorized to conduct attack sorties against North Vietnam and Laos as necessary to accomplish assigned missions".[10]

Restrictions against strikes within the Hanoi prohibited circle and in the CHICOM buffer zone were removed by JCS in August. The CHICOM buffer zone was the area within 30-NM of the Chinese border from the border of Laos eastward to 106° east longitude and within 25-NM of the Chinese border from 106° east longitude to the Gulf of Tonkin. The Hanoi prohibited area was the area within 10-NM of the center of Hanoi (210137N-1055121E). The Hanoi restricted area was the area within 30-NM of the center of Hanoi, excluding the Hanoi prohibited area. The Haiphong prohibited area was the area within 4-NM of the center of Haiphong (205122N-106411OE). The Haiphong restricted area was the area within 10-NM of the center of Haiphong, excluding the Haiphong prohibited area. The authority to strike rail targets in the CHICOM buffer zone created the opportunity to interdict or destroy war supplies as far away from the battlefield as possible, and thereby decreased the quantity of these supplies which would eventually reach their destination. The JCS stipulated that every feasible precaution was to be taken in conducting these airstrikes to preclude penetration of the CHICOM border and to avoid engagements with CHICOM MIGs, except in self-defense over NVN territory. The precautions were to include the use of experienced pilots, adequate electronic capability to insure positive navigational control, and, if feasible, positive strike control. Targets were to be attacked only when weather conditions would enable positive identification of the target. In addition, JCS authorized CINCPAC to conduct armed recon against LOC and LOC-associated targets in the Haiphong restricted area.[11/]

Plans for exploitation of the buffer zone target system along the northeast railroad included both Air Force and Navy aircraft. The two services coordinated the strikes to achieve maximum surprise and destruction of bridges and marshalling yards before the NVN could achieve a threatening defensive posture. Approximately 250 attack sorties were flown against selected LOC targets in the buffer zone during August with the result that 250 pieces of rolling stock were destroyed or damaged. The LOC segment extensions within the Hanoi and Haiphong 10-mile restricted areas, plus the add-on targets, exposed approximately 135 additional targets to armed recon operations. In the Hanoi circle, 24 fixed LOC target elements were attacked with more than 300 sorties. 12/

With the authorization of strikes in the Hanoi prohibited circle and in the CHICOM buffer zone, the importance of Phuc Yen airfield as a target increased significantly, both militarily and psychologically. CINCPAC pointed out to the CJCS that NVN was undoubtedly aware of Phuc Yen's immunity from attack, since the Air Order of Battle (AOB) carried 20 of the 27 MIGs presently in country at Phuc Yen. It was also believed that most of the NVN aviation fuel was located there, and there was evidence of a supply depot only two miles north of the runway. In requesting authority to strike Phuc Yen, CINCPAC stated that attacks against it would remove Phuc Yen as a refuge, and also force enemy fighter aircraft to operate out of other NVN airfields with less adequate facilities for sustained operations or out of Communist China. 13/

The F-4D, Walleye modified aircraft, which had arrived in SEA in July, flew its first mission on 14 August. The AGM-62 Walleye was an air-to-surface, homing glide weapon incorporating an automatic contrast tracking television guidance system. Suitable targets were bridges, structures, and similar areas which provided the necessary contrast. On their 14 August mission, two aircraft flying in formation released their bombs simultaneously and destroyed a 250-foot dock. The initial targets for Walleye strikes were hand-picked for good contrast, and missions were carried out in areas of light defenses and good weather. Subsequently, less selectivity was exercised in the employment

of this weapon and its effectiveness was downgraded. From August through
8 November, when the program was suspended for reassessment, Walleye had hit
14 targets and launched 22 missiles. Thirteen missiles had hit their target,
two were near misses and caused possible damage, and seven missed. Of those
targets struck, six bridges were destroyed; two were damaged; and one
received possible damage from a near miss. Four buildings were destroyed
and four damaged; one pier was damaged; and one barge sunk.[14/]

Of the 63 targets authorized ROLLING THUNDER executed on 21 July, 21
remained unstruck as of 30 September. Eight of these were in the Hanoi
prohibited area and were not attacked because of the strike restrictions
promulgated on 19 August and in effect throughout September. Poor weather
caused diversions and cancellations of strikes on the other 13 targets. The
enemy thus had an opportunity to repair rail lines and bridges. For instance,
the Doumer Bridge, linking Hanoi to the northeast and east, had been severely
damaged in the strike of 11 August. At first, NVN was forced to resort to
ferries and pontoon bridges; but by September, the bridge had been repaired
to the point that a near-normal rate of material handling might be possible.
However, the constant pressure forced the enemy to employ a costly time
delaying shuttle system. Supplies were offloaded at points of disruption, and
then either reloaded onto rail cars further down the line or transported to
their destination by trucks.[15/]

The rail interdiction campaign had steadily increased North Vietnam's
costs for transshipment of needed supplies. In May, 152,000 short tons
required transshipment to by-pass all interdictions and outages on the

northeast railroad (approximately 50,000 truck loads); by August, this figure had increased to 259,000 short tons (approximately 86,000 truck loads); and in the period 1 - 20 September, 171,000 short tons (approximately 57,000 truck loads) required transshipment. Equipment and supplies were concentrated along Route 4 in North Vietnam, about seven kilometers west of Dong Dang near the Chinese border; a nearby area contained numerous storage buildings and extensive open storage. North Vietnam might have been attempting to overcome transportation difficulties caused by recent interdiction of the Hanoi-Dong rail line by diverting rail cargo to highway transport. There was reportedly heavy congestion at Haiphong Port and open storage on roads and under trees in the city parks. Most of the port work was accomplished during hours of darkness and port processing appeared to have generally deteriorated. [16]

The unfavorable weather in the northern areas during September caused diverts to RP I. In an effort to destroy enemy artillery and rocket positions firing on friendly positions south of the DMZ, Operation NEUTRALIZE was implemented in that area on 11 September. Commando Sabre aircraft, call sign Misty, had an active role in this operation and proved effective in pinpointing field artillery positions. [17]

The 7AF had started MK-36 seeding operations in RP I and Laos at the end of July. By the end of September, analysis showed that routes of travel in the panhandle area had been altered to avoid seeded areas, although there was no actual assessment of damage inflicted. the MK-36 Destructor was an adaptation of an existing weapon, the MK-82 General Purpose bomb with the high drag Snakeye fin. An arming device and a firing mechanism were attached to

9

the MK-82 500-pound bomb, which gave it the capability to function as a water mine. Since the nature of the MK-36 made it difficult to determine results on targets in hostile areas, it was believed the effects could be more readily assessed if future employment were restricted to fewer target areas, which were periodically reseeded. Therefore, five primary ferry links connecting principal north-south LOCs (Xuan Son, Huu Hung, and Mi Le ferry complexes and Quang Khe and Phuong Chay highway ferries), were identified as areas where the stoppage or diversion could be more rapidly identified and designated as targets for future operations. 18/

The limited lethal radius and easy detection of the MK-36 limited its effectiveness against land LOCs, although it had some value from the harassment standpoint. In early September, CINCPAC directed that the MK-36 would be employed primarily in water LOCs, pending further testing of its effectiveness on land. There was also little information, however, that positively identified the effectiveness of the MK-36 along North Vietnam's water LOCs. 19/

Beginning in October, the Air Force F-4s joined Marine and Navy aircraft in conducting seeding operations along the Red River. This waterway had increased in importance since the successful interdiction of rail traffic on the northwest railroad, which ran generally parallel to the river. Since these routes were heavily defended and could not be kept under adequate surveillance, it was difficult to evaluate the effectiveness of seeding efforts. According to one Intelligence report, the North Vietnamese were aware that mines had been dropped in their rivers and they had caused "great difficulty" with river traffic, especially between Hanoi and Haiphong. The same report stated that the mines had not been removed because the North Vietnamese Navy was not familiar with minesweeping methods. Seeded water areas had been monitored on an infrequent basis, but no actual detonations or debris had been observed.[20]

CINCPAC informed JCS in October that, in his opinion, the best evaluation of the MK-36 effectiveness would be accomplished in CONUS under controlled test conditions. When all of the characteristics of the weapon were known, its use could be optimized and known factors applied to any combat evaluation. The CINCPAC recommended that:[21]

- Production of the MK-36 be increased to the approved production base of 15,000 per month.
- Testing and evaluation of the MK-36 be continued and expanded.
- Adaptation of M-117, MK-83, and MK-84 to DST usage be expedited.

As a result of more favorable weather in October, airstrike activity in North Vietnam increased. Also, the suspension of airstrikes against authorized targets in the 10-NM Hanoi prohibited area and against Phuc Yen airfield were cancelled. USAF flew 1,309 sorties out of a total of 1,544 in RP VIA, and 130 out of 1,651 in VIB, averaging 43 sorties per day. On 7 October, eight F-105s made 30 strafing passes at Hoa Luc Airfield, which resulted in four Hound and two Hook helicopters destroyed. Phuc Yen, the major military airfield in North Vietnam, was attacked by the USN and USAF on 24 October. Another attack was made on 25 October, which included the use of Walleye glide bombs--one Walleye making a direct hit on the control tower. The two-day strikes destroyed and damaged five MIG-21s and seven MIG-15/17s. During the period 25-30 October, 111 sorties attacked the Hanoi railroad and highway bridges over the Red River and Canal des Rapides (JCS 12 and 13). The strikes removed these bridges from the LOC system and forced NVN to turn to the inefficient, time-consuming ferry system. In anticipation of this move, the USAF and USN emplaced MK-36 bombs in the areas of the ferries.[22]

The increased activity brought heavy losses to the 388th Tactical Fighter Wing (TFW) during the first week of October, and caused concern both to the Wing Commander and the 7AF Commander. During that week, the Wing lost six aircraft and five crews (one crew was recovered); in addition, 11 aircraft were damaged. Both the Wing and 7AF explored various avenues to decrease the loss rate, including tactical formation changes; improved ground controlled intercept (GCI) and warning capability, and interdiction of rail lines at more numerous points. A daily variation in fragging, from multiple cuts to prime point targets, was also considered. The Commander, 7AF, stated that procedures and tactics were to be improved and refined to achieve optimum strike effectiveness with minimum losses.[23]

In response to a request from JCS, 7AF recommended an optimum air campaign against North Vietnam for a twelve-month period beginning in November 1967. The 7AF plan submitted to PACAF placed emphasis on keeping the northeast, the Hanoi-Thai Nguyen-Kep triangle, and the northwest railroads interdicted, and the associated transshipment points and railroad yards unserviceable. This was to include destruction of locomotives and rolling stock, and major supply storage and handling facilities. If authorization were granted to strike related targets in the currently restricted Hanoi/Haiphong areas on a selective basis, it would help to isolate Hanoi and Haiphong from obtaining and distributing material from external sources. [24/]

In the lower Route Package, particularly RP I, air operations would be directed toward preventing a buildup of enemy forces and supplies to support a major campaign, and to reduce the pressure against friendly forces opposite the DMZ. Efforts in Laos would be directed toward inflicting heavy losses on the enemy infiltration lines, and inhibiting the flow of supplies and materials into and through the area. [25/]

The major effort during the NE monsoon season would be in the STEEL TIGER area, with a shift to RP I during the SW monsoon. The aircraft fragged for RP V and VI targets would be diverted from assigned targets in BARREL ROLL or other areas when weather conditions dictated. [26/] All forces would be controlled through the Airborne Battlefield Command and Control Centers (ABCCCs), and could be quickly diverted from their assigned targets to lucrative fleeting targets, when warranted, to include diversions to Navy Route Packages. [27/]

The current level of reconnaissance effort would be maintained during the November 1967 - November 1968 period. Efforts would continue to increase availability of low-level drone-type capability, which would materially enhance intelligence-gathering capability, conserve the reconnaissance aircraft force, and improve the effectiveness of airstrikes. [28/]

Single-ship Commando Nail F-105 strikes would be primarily directed against targets in RP V and VI in a night harassment role, supplemented by Marine A-6s and by the F-111s when available. The use of the F-4D and possibly the F-111 in a pathfinder role would be expanded during this period. MSQ would also be employed to provide strike capability in all areas during non-VFR weather.[29]

MUSCLE SHOALS, the air-supported anti-infiltration system, might provide a new source of real-time intelligence and could be a major factor in the conduct of the interdiction campaign in this area. Initial dedicated aircraft sortie allocation would average 12 per day, increasing to approximately 40 per day beginning the first quarter of calendar year 1968. ECM support, tankers, intelligence gathering systems, communications, and other support of strike operations would be continued at approximately the current level of effort with adjustments as required.[30]

In commenting on an optimum air campaign against North Vietnam for the period November 1967 - November 1968, CINCPAC pointed out to JCS that denying entry of war supplies into NVN would be far more effective in impeding the war effort, than any later actions to interdict movement of supplies west and south. Sea imports constituted about 80 percent of the total imports, and without them Hanoi could not continue the war for a protracted period. CINCPAC recommended removal of the restrictions against mining of the major deep water ports and the prohibited areas around Hanoi and Haiphong; reduction of the CHICOM buffer zone to 15 miles; and unrestricted attacks against the northeast and northwest rail lines and roads. After imported war supplies had been dispersed within NVN, a much greater effort was required to interdict the movement southward. Armed recon strikes on key interdiction points and seeding of LOCs southward in conjunction with the isolation of Hanoi and Haiphong would be required. Strikes against North Vietnam's air defense control facilities, all jet-capable airfields, and SAM and AAA sites were also recommended.[31]

CINCPAC informed JCS that an advance static allocation of sorties in Route Packages was not feasible due to weather factors, degree of destruction of target systems, effectiveness of LOC's interdiction, and generation of new targets. To apply strike and armed recon effort when and where needed, operational flexibility was required in NVN and Laos.[32]

Although 7AF did not receive any direct comment from JCS on its 12-month optimum air campaign, certain restrictions were lifted even prior to the proposed November implementation date; i.e., authorization to strike Phuc Yen airfield.

ROLLING THUNDER continued during November, but adverse weather limited the number of sorties. LOCs remained the prime target and received the greatest weight of effort in the northern areas. Due to weather diverts from this area, USAF flew 2,238 out of 3,771 sorties in RP I. The use of COMBAT SKYSPOT permitted the delivery of ordnance in RP I regardless of the weather. The Ron Ferry complex and Quang Khe Highway Ferry were seeded with MK-36. As of 30 November, 4,784 destructors had been emplaced throughout NVN; 1,763 by USAF and 3,021 by USN.[33]

The large amount of ordnance being jettisoned as a result of targets not acquired in RP V and VI was once again the subject of discussion. Ordnance was jettisoned safe in uninhabited areas and the Gulf of Tonkin, to avoid collateral damage to non-military targets. CINCPACAF believed that continuous study of all available possibilities should lead to options which would reduce or eliminate present non-productive jettisoning procedures. In November, 7AF informed CINCPACAF that additional pressure was being placed on units to reduce jettison rates. The designation of alternate targets for armed reconnaissance in Route Package V along the LOCs had again been directed. Also, the primary target was backed up with an alternate armed reconnaissance attack; and if that was questionable, an MSQ attack would be the automatic form of bombing. When weather was unsuitable for armed reconnaissance attacks, priority would initially go to Hoa Lac, Kep, and Phuc Yen airfields followed by Kep and Thai Nguyen and other marshaling yards. Radar (Commando Nail) would be assigned as augmentation to morning MSQ missions for afternoon strikes in Route Package V. Seventh Air Force would continue to work with the Navy on significant radar targets in Route Package VIB. 34/

The weather over NVN during December was typical for that time of the year--generally low ceilings, restrictive visibilities, and rain. The adverse weather combined with the 24-hour Christmas standdown resulted in reduced air activity. The Hanoi Railroad and Highway Bridge over the Red River (JCS 12.00), and the Hanoi Railroad and Highway Bridge over the Canal des Rapides (JCS 13.00) had been dropped in October, but were repaired and apparently serviceable by mid-November. JCS 12.00 was hit again on 14 December, and both road and rail beds were rendered unserviceable. On 18 December, 32 F-105s struck the bridge using 750- and 3000-pound bombs. It was estimated that three-to-four weeks would be required to repair the damage. 35/

During the Christmas cease-fire period (24 December, 1800H - 25 December, 1800H), normal armed reconnaissance and airstrike operations were ordered suspended in NVN. Intensified aerial reconnaissance and BLUE TREE operations would be conducted in the DMZ and in Route Package I. If authorized by COMUSMACV or CINCPAC, airstrikes and artillery fire could be conducted against observed, abnormally great military resupply activity in NVN south of 20 degrees north latitude, and against targets in NVN that posed an immediate and direct threat to friendly forces. 36/

The 12-NM restriction on immediate pursuit into the CHICOM buffer zone was changed in December. The CINCPAC message stated that: 37/

> *"Aircraft engaged in immediate pursuit are authorized to pursue enemy aircraft into restricted and/or prohibited areas; however, pursuit is not, repeat, is not authorized into the territorial airspace of Communist China. Every precaution will be taken to prevent violation of the CHICOM border. When engaged in immediate pursuit in connection with affording protection to strike forces, U.S. forces are not authorized to strike NVN air bases from which aircraft may be operating if the airbase had not been previously struck. However, this does not prohibit attacking the pursued airborne aircraft."*

CHAPTER II

CLOSE AIR SUPPORT

At midyear, close air support was concentrated in I Corps, which was the scene of the heaviest enemy activity. Air Force, Marine, and Navy tactical aircraft, and B-52s pounded positions in and north of the DMZ around-the-clock to silence them. Operation NEUTRALIZE was initiated in September for the specific purpose of degrading the effectiveness of enemy artillery/rocket positions in that area. By October, airpower, Marine and Navy artillery, and the monsoon weather had combined to significantly reduce NVA/VC pressure on USMC outposts around the DMZ. [1]

In November, VC/NVA forces reversed their former reluctance to commit their forces to large-scale battles, as evidenced by the battles of Loc Ninh and Dak To. But following this attempt to fight set-piece battles, the enemy reverted to guerrilla hit and run/ambush during search and destroy operations where Free World Forces invaded known VC/NVA-controlled areas. [2]

During the period July - December 1967, the Air Force flew a total of 62,200 combat sorties in-country, 46,800 of which were close air support. It delivered approximately 95,000 tons of ordnance during this same period and destroyed or damaged 50,000 structures and 4,500 sampans. The USAF lost a total of 86 aircraft, in-country, during the second half of 1967; 56 of them combat aircraft. This compared to a loss of 68 aircraft (39 combat) during the period January - June 1967. [3] (Appendix I - V.)

COMBAT DRAGON

The introduction of A-37s into CAS operations and the use of jet aircraft in a FAC role were new developments, which increased the effectiveness of tactical air support during the second half of 1967. Operations to demonstrate the feasibility of utilizing jet aircraft in the performance of the FAC role were started on 30 June under the code name COMMANDO SABRE. F-100F Misty aircraft were used in lieu of O-1 and O-2 aircraft, which were too vulnerable in high-threat areas such as RP I and TALLY HO. The Misty aircraft flew at altitudes of about 5,000 feet, with missions averaging four and one-half hours duration. By marking targets and directing the fighter aircraft to the target, they increased the effectiveness of strike aircraft and also reduced fighter exposure time to enemy defenses. During Operation NEUTRALIZE, these aircraft played an active role by directing strikes against enemy field artillery firing on friendly forces located just south of the DMZ. [4/]

The A-37s provided effective air support during the battles of Loc Ninh, Dak To, and Bu Dop. These aircraft, which arrived in Vietnam in July, were designed to meet specific requirements of the USAF for counterinsurgency operations and close air support for ground forces. They are twin-jet aircraft with a maximum speed of 478 miles per hour and can carry 4,855 pounds of ordnance; they are equipped with one 7.62-mm nose-mounted minigun. [5/]

Under the code name COMBAT DRAGON, A-37 combat missions were initiated from Bien Hoa on 15 August, by a newly-formed combat evaluation detachment. By 30 September, the squadron had logged 1,673 sorties. The combat analysis of the A-37 as a counterinsurgency weapons system hit its peak during

October and November. During October alone, 1,614 sorties were flown for an average of 52 per day. Operational experience proved the A-37 was capable of fast turn around and quick response to any immediate call for a sustained length of time.[6/]

In addition to Operation NEUTRALIZE in the DMZ area, the second half of 1967 was characterized by the dramatic battles of Dak To and Loc Ninh in II and III Corps. For the first time since the A Shau and Ia Drang Valley battles of April and May 1965, the enemy was willing to engage in sustained battles. While these battles were tactical successes for Allied forces, the enemy gained a strategic advantage by turning Allied attention toward the border and away from the cities which were to become the targets of the VC TET attacks. In late 1967, planning for the massive TET Offensive required the expansion and extension of logistical movements into South Vietnam. As pointed out by the 7AF Directorate of Intelligence:[7/]

> *"Movements of such a magnitude could not remain undetected, and, once detected, would be subjected to massive air interdiction. In such a situation, classical communist doctrine called for a diversion-- Loc Ninh, Bu Dop, and Dak To followed; all fiercely fought; each causing substantial diversion of U.S. and Free World Forces."*

According to a high-ranking defector who rallied to the GVN on 19 April 1968, the purpose of the battles of Loc Ninh and Dak To was to build enemy morale by fighting and to gain combat experience. The attacks were reportedly authorized at the insistent request of the enemy unit commanders on the battlefield. The higher level cadre allegedly did not approve of these attacks, since it was evident to them that they would be bloody and useless.[8/]

Loc Ninh

On 29 October 1967, the enemy attacked the district town of Loc Ninh, 72 miles north of Saigon in Binh Long Province. During this nine-day battle, the attacking Communist forces suffered a major defeat, and the casualties they sustained during the determined effort to overrun a relatively insignificant outpost were seemingly far out of proportion to the value of their target. The enemy suffered 852 KIA compared to 50 friendly losses. Air support contributing to this significant engagement consisted of F-4Cs, F-100s, A-37s, B-52s, and B-57s, strafing and bombing the enemy continuously. Reconnaissance missions were flown day and night, using RF-4Cs, RF-101s, and RB-57s. From 29 October through 7 November, 452 close air support sorties, 21 Spooky, 35 COMBAT SKYSPOT, 8 ARC LIGHT, and numerous reconnaissance and airlift missions were flown. 9/

At the time of the attack, elements of two South Vietnamese Regional Forces companies and one Popular Forces platoon with two American NCO advisors were at Loc Ninh. One kilometer to the south was a South Vietnamese Special Forces Camp with six U.S. Special Forces advisors assigned to three Civilian Irregular Defense Group companies. These isolated local forces relayed any requests for tactical air support, including emergency airlift, through the Tactical Air Control Parties (TACPs) assigned to ARVN and U.S. Infantry divisions in the area. 10/

At 0115 hours on 29 October 1967, an estimated enemy force of 1,500 attacked the District Subsector Headquarters compound with mortar, heavy ground fire, and 40-mm anti-tank rockets. At approximately 0200 hours, two enemy battalions struck the compound and the Special Forces Camp, penetrating the northern half of the compound. Fighting bunker to bunker, the Regional Force units were forced to withdraw to the southern half of the compound area. An U.S. advisor, the District Chief, and one squad remained in the command bunker. Control of the command post permitted communication between the ground and the FACs throughout the night and helped to insure the close coordination necessary to put ordnance along the camp perimeters. 11/

When the Phuoc Long Sector FAC arrived about 0230 hours, the defenders were receiving mortar fire from all directions, with the heaviest fire coming from the rubber trees east of the runway. The District Chief directed antipersonnel ordnance and artillery onto his now exposed position, a deep concrete bunker, which was built to withstand and deflect explosions. Spooky (the AC-47) and artillery poured ordnance onto the bunker and kept the enemy away until reinforcements arrived. 12/

The reinforced defenders counterattacked to regain the northern part of the subsector compound, and succeeded in driving out the enemy troops. Only sporadic contacts were made during the following morning as damaged fortifications were repaired and patrol activities resumed. At 0500H on 31 October, the enemy launched a major assault. Within minutes a minigun-armed C-47 Spooky, and an armed helicopter were en route to assist the defenders. The enemy employed human wave assaults from the west, north, and south. Army artillery situated at the south end of the airstrip, placed direct line fire into the enemy coming from the rubber trees and moving west across the airstrip.

The defenders began to run low on ammunition after fighting off five separate attempts to overrun the compound. In this critical situation, one Army officer described the role of tactical air as follows:[13]

> *"If it hadn't been for air, we would have lost this place. The air chopped them up at the wires. My men had about 30 rounds of ammunition left per man when the attackers were driven off, never having broken the perimeter. They came right down our perimeter with cannons, antipersonnel mines, and then when the enemy began pulling back, they hit them with high explosive stuff."*

By 0700 hours, the compound and the area around District Headquarters was cleared of the enemy and airlifted supplies began to arrive. On 1 November, enemy activity was reduced, with only sporadic contacts throughout the day.

The enemy renewed his attack on 2 November at 0045 hours, striking the compound, Special Forces Camp, 18th Infantry positions, and both ends of the runway. Within ten minutes, one FAC, C-47 flareships, and two light fire teams were on station; additional FACs were en route. During the next five hours, the enemy made at least three unsuccessful assaults using mass forces, heavy ground fire, and mortars. Despite intense antiaircraft fire from .50-caliber weapons, tactical air support flew a record number of sorties, inflicting heavy casualties.[14]

At 2220 hours on 3 November, enemy forces launched their last concentrated attack six kilometers northeast of Loc Ninh, using small-arms, automatic weapons, .50-caliber machine guns, and mortars. Flareships, tactical air, and light fire teams were called in; and, by 0400 hours, all firing had ended. Throughout the remainder of the day, only small engagements took place in the Loc Ninh area. During the next three days, search and destroy missions, resulting in small engagements, were conducted in the Loc Ninh area by U.S. forces. The last enemy action against Loc Ninh took place on 6 November at 1825H, when the enemy fired 20 rounds of 60-mm mortar fire against defensive positions. Despite their claims to the contrary, the battle of Loc Ninh was a costly and humiliating defeat for the enemy. 15/

Dak To

A similar action took place at the Special Forces Camp at Dak To, in the central highlands of II Corps, during the period 4 - 23 November. Dak To blocked a convenient entry route into South Vietnam, and the enemy hoped to neutralize it by mounting rocket and mortar attacks from the high hills surrounding the airstrip. An enemy offensive with large scale engagements had been expected in this area since October. To counter the enemy buildup, U.S. troops were pulled from populated areas into this remote border region. This move unwittingly gave the enemy greater freedom to prepare for the TET Offensive against the cities. 16/

Allied forces began moving units into the area around Dak To, a small village in Kontum Province, on 1 November. At 1230 hours on 4 November, two companies of the U.S. 3d Battalion, 12th Infantry, made contact five kilometers south of Dak To, with an estimated enemy battalion. During the next two days, 74 tactical air sorties and 15 ARC LIGHT sorties were flown in the area, as the enemy increased his pressure. For the next week and a half, heavy, sporadic engagements continued each time friendly forces encountered enemy defensive positions in the rugged terrain. The effect of airstrikes on the enemy became apparent on 7 November, when tactical air sorties resulted in two secondary explosions and possibly 100 KIA. From 8 to 14 November, an additional 354 tactical air sorties were flown. 17/

On 14 November, the enemy succeeded in disrupting US/ARVN resupply efforts with mortar attacks on Dak To airfield, which was located approximately five kilometers southwest of Dak To. The airfield had a 4,200 foot hard surface runway and was flanked by U.S. and ARVN Civilian Irregular Defense Group (CIDG) forces to the east and west. The initial enemy barrage caught three C-130s on the ground, two of which were destroyed and the third received major damage. Three O-1s parked on the ramp received minor damage. The ammunition supply point also took several direct hits and burned out of control throughout the day and night, its massive explosions closing the airstrip. The airstrip was cleared the following day and reopened on 17 November, with the restriction of only one C-130 on the ground at any one time. 18/

In the pitched battles fought to clear VC/NVA troops from heavily fortified hilltop positions surrounding and dominating the Dak To base camp, tactical air support proved extremely valuable. The dense, multi-canopied jungle sometimes made it necessary to use heavy general purpose bombs against enemy fortifications to clear an area, so that napalm could reach the bunker positions. Tactical air was also used, chiefly by the Army, to cut landing zones for air assaults and medical evacuations. Heavy ordnance and antipersonnel cluster bombs were too dangerous for use when the enemy was in close contact with friendly forces. Tactics called for ground troops to make contact, pull back and call in air and artillery, and then return to the contact area. As the Dak To battle progressed, the effectiveness of these tactics was attested to by ground commanders who became more willing to call in close air support, and to shut off their artillery cover to permit access to the target.[19/]

The most common aircraft load was napalm and 750-pound bombs. Napalm was used for precision placement of ordnance for very close air support. The destruction of enemy fortifications and landing zones required heavy bombs. The conflicting requirements for explosive power and napalm occasionally caught the Air Force short of heavy ordnance. More preplanning would have allowed more fighter sorties, and would also have lessened the delay in getting the ordnance desired, since there would have been less downloading of aircraft to achieve the right load mix. However, the obvious inability to anticipate all enemy action limited the utilization of a high ratio of pre-planned sorties.[20/]

A total of 2,096 close air support sorties were flown in support of U.S. and ARVN forces in the battle for Dak To, nearly all by the Air Force.

	Missions Requested	Missions Flown	Sorties Flown
FAC Preplanned	529	481	957
FAC Immediate	498	496	1,011
COMBAT SKYSPOT Preplanned	60	48	49
COMBAT SKYSPOT Immediate	20	13	17
Spooky	65	62	62
TOTAL	1,172	1,100	2,096

In flying those sorties, one Air Force aircraft was destroyed on 19 November eight kilometers east of Dak To Special Forces Camp. The number two aircraft of an F-4 flight followed the lead into a target delivering napalm and crashed in the target area. The pilot was recovered, but the aircraft commander was missing.[21/]

Friendly losses included 283 U.S. and 61 South Vietnamese killed versus 1,644 enemy killed. An estimated 544 enemy were killed by air, along with 177 bunkers destroyed and 138 secondary explosions or fires touched off. These figures, however, give only a partial picture of the destruction caused by tactical air, since some enemy sites were beyond recognition, and the enemy often policed sites before friendly troops could reach the area.[22/]

The following remarks made by 4th Infantry Division personnel in their After Action Report were typical of the comments praising tactical air support during the battle of Dak To:[23/]

> *"Tactical air was used to the maximum in support of ground forces in contact with a disciplined, well-equipped and well-trained enemy who chose to stand and fight from heavily fortified positions....The spirit and dedication of the U.S. Air Force to give close and continuous tactical air support to the ground forces can best be described by the fact some pilots flew three and four sorties in one day. Considering the flight time, time over target, and rearming of the aircraft, this is a tremendous feat. Forward Air Controllers spent eight to ten hours a day over target areas, landing only to tactically rearm with rockets and refuel. Night time was virtually non-existent as flares from Spooky aircraft were used to permit the FACs to see their targets. Tactical air support was close and continuous regardless of the time or place."*

Bo Duc

In a third major assault on fortified positions close to the Cambodian border, an estimated reinforced enemy battalion attacked Bo Duc, a District Headquarters in Phuoc Long Province and Bu Dop, the Special Forces CIDG Camp four kilometers to the north, in the early morning hours of 29 November. The well-coordinated and imaginative assault on Bo Duc failed due to tactical air, which put ordnance within 20 feet of Allied positions and kept the enemy at bay, and the heavy barrage of fire put on them by more than a dozen Army light fire teams.[24/]

During the next 11 days, the enemy made repeated rocket and mortar attacks against Bo Dop/Bo Duc, putting in more than 600 rounds on friendly positions. On 8 December, the enemy made two final ground attacks on night positions of U.S. units and then withdrew, ending the offensive in the immediate area. Parting enemy attacks were made on Dak Son, near Song Be, killing 74 Montagnards, and on a U.S. battalion near An Loc, killing one American and 124 enemy. Then the offensive in Binh Luong and Phuoc Long ended and the enemy left the region, moving southward into War Zone C.[25/]

Enemy Counter-Air Tactics

The VC/NVA have adopted both passive and active defense measures to counter the threat posed to them, in-country, by aerial reconnaissance, and the associated follow-up airstrikes. They have developed an extensive system of foxholes, bunkers, trenches, tunnels, caves, and AA gun emplacements throughout areas under their control, or in contested areas. In addition to elaborate underground fortifications, the VC/NVA have turned increasingly to dispersion of supplies, facilities, and units, plus the extensive and skillful use of camouflage for protection. 26/

Enemy units operated an aircraft warning system based on visual sightings and radio intercept, and used this information to limit or minimize the effects of airstrikes. In addition, they used spurious English and Vietnamese language radio transmissions to misdirect airstrikes. Although the warning system was not sophisticated and varied between units in the degree of implementation, it extended down to guerrilla units, while the use of spurious radio transmissions extended down to VC Local Force battalion level. Interrogation reports and captured documents attested to its effectiveness in many instances; for example, the enemy allegedly learned about operations in the Iron Triangle one month prior to their beginning. Basic to the VC/NVA aircraft warning system was the use of radios captured from ground forces and those recovered from downed aircraft. Communist China and Russia served as the second major source of supply for audio equipment. 27/

According to USMACV J-2 PERINTREP dated 20 May 1967: 28/

> *"Communications intelligence is perhaps the fastest growing facet of the VC intelligence effort--VC foreknowledge of GVN/US/FWMAF military operations, including airstrikes, may stem from the intercept of friendly cleartext radio communications. Based on communications intercept capability, the VC have successfully avoided military sweeps and airstrikes, have set up ambushes against friendly elements, and have even conducted radio deception operations such as luring strike aircraft and medevac helicopters into ambush."*

Captured documents revealed VC/NVA awareness of the necessity for counter air tactics. The two central themes in current VC/NVA tactics designed to counter the threat of airstrikes during maneuver and combat operations were: (1) stay close to the enemy; and (2) deceive or divert airstrikes. In the first case, proximity prevented artillery and airpower employment against the VC/NVA, except as a last resort. The rationale behind the second theme was that it was expedient to expose or sacrifice a small element to protect the main body and permit it to carry out its mission. [29]

Night movements, assaults, and retreats were basic enemy tactics designed to prevent the application of airpower against large units. For defense against aerial reconnaissance and airstrikes, the VC/NVA relied heavily on the cover of darkness. When enemy units traveled or conducted operations during daylight hours, maximum use was made of routes which were concealed from aerial observation by the tree canopy and other jungle growth. Vegetation was also used for individual camouflage. In both day and night combat, the VC/NVA units attempted to draw the fire of aircraft to their own dispersed AA positions, to dummy AA positions and to dummy battlegrounds. VC/NVA units prepared fortified and camouflaged positions at the battleground and along planned withdrawal routes. They also endeavored to smother smoke markers and fire false smoke markers in order to misdirect airstrikes. [30]

CHAPTER III

TACTICAL AIR RECONNAISSANCE

Reconnaissance Force Structure

The primary reconnaissance effort in Southeast Asia in July 1967 consisted of the photo reconnaissance force of RF-4Cs and RF-101s located at two SEA bases, Tan Son Nhut AB in South Vietnam, and at Udorn RTAFB in Thailand. At Tan Son Nhut, the 460th Tactical Reconnaissance Wing had 35 RF-4Cs and 12 RF-101s, while the 432d TRW had 25 RF-4Cs and 15 RF-101s at Udorn. The USAF electronic intelligence fleet of ten EB-66Cs and nine EB-66Bs were stationed at Takhli, Thailand, with the prime missions of ELINT/ECM over NVN. The remainder of the force was made up of three RB-57s at Tan Son Nhut and 45 EC-47s at three bases in South Vietnam - 16 at TSN, 15 at Nha Trang, and 14 at Pleiku. These aircraft provided Airborne Radio Direction Finding (ARDF), operations against enemy-operated transmitters in South Vietnam, and over the more permissive areas of Laos. 1/

The overall reconnaissance force structure changed considerably in the six month-period ending in December, 1967 (Fig. 1). In August, the first EB-66E joined the Takhli EB fleet. The EB-66E, a modified "RB" model, with all threat-frequency jamming and increased power for its electronic function, was scheduled to replace the old EB-66B in the 41st and 42d Tactical Electronic Warfare Squadron (TEWS) under the 355th TFW at that base. By the end of September, five "E" models were in operation and one of the "B"s had been withdrawn for modification. As of 31 October, the numbers of aircraft roughly equaled each other--six "E"s and eight "B"s--but not until November did the number of EB-66E sorties begin to approach those of the EB-66B. By the end of December, however, 13 of the "E" models were in place and flew 214 sorties for the month as against 132 for the three EB-66s there. The "B" models, in the meantime, were being remodified to give them EWO-operated jamming equipment of similar power and frequency coverage as the EB-66E. The EB-66C resources (PECM aircraft with reduced active ECM capability) remained stable at nine to ten aircraft throughout the period.[2/]

Another significant move, in addition to the deployment of EB-66Es to Takhli, was that of the replacement of RF-101s in Thailand with RF-4Cs. On 30 October, the 14th TRS, consisting of 16 RF-4Cs from Bergstrom AFB, Texas, closed at Udorn RTAFB and were assigned to the 432d TRW at that base. Two days later, on 1 November, the 20th TRS at Udorn was officially deactivated. A portion of its RF-101s were assigned to the 45th TRS at Tan Son Nhut; the remainder were returned to the States. This move provided the Thai-based reconnaissance force with the faster and more sophisticated RF-4C for the high threat Route Packages of NVN, while the older RF-101 took over a larger proportion of the effort in the more permissive areas of NVN and Laos, and in South Vietnam.[3/]

In a move to provide increased imagery to users, the 460th TRW instituted a 60-to-90-day test of a partial Photo Processing and Interpretation Facility (PPIF) at Phu Cat AB in northern II CTZ, South Vietnam. Missions departing Tan Son Nhut for targets in the northern CTZs were afforded longer loiter time over their target areas. Instead of returning to TSN following each sortie, the aircraft could land at Phu Cat and download the film for

TACTICAL RECONNAISSANCE ASSETS
SEA
(As of 31 Dec 67)

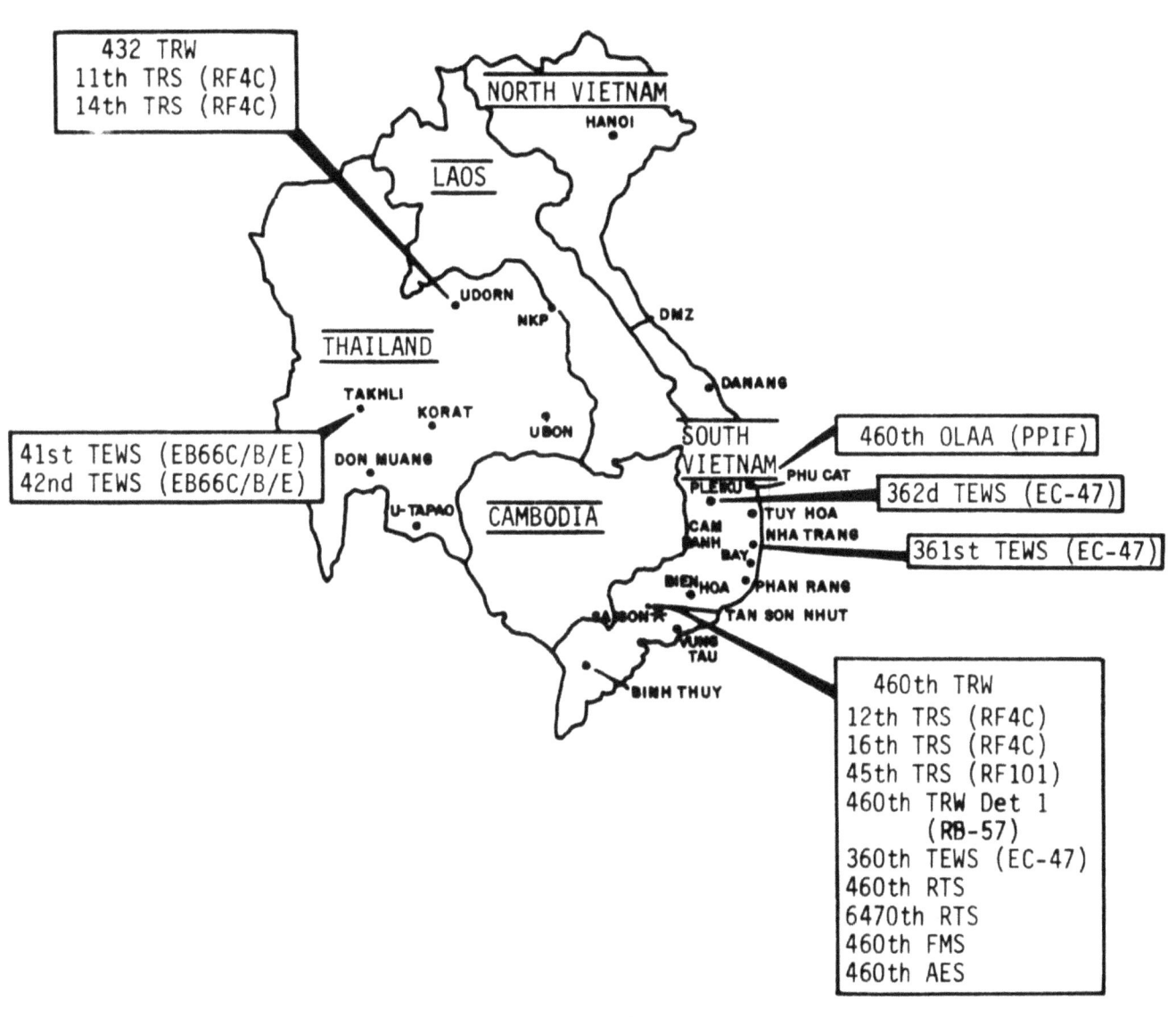

FIGURE 1

processing. While the aircraft was being turned around for a second in-country mission, wet-print readouts of significant intelligence data could already be Immediate Photo Interpretation Reported; Hot Items would be sent out immediately by telephonic means or by teletype. The first advantage noted was a 30-to-40 minute increase in time over target in the critical I and II Corps areas. The test program began 6 August and, on 15 October, it was approved as a permanent PPIF. As of the end of December, the facility at Phu Cat was processing an average of seven in-country missions per day. 4/

Changes in Operating Procedures over NVN

Because of the high incidence of radar-directed guns and SA-2s in NVN, a change of operating procedures was instituted by 7AF on 3 August. From that date, all reconnaissance aircraft flying into the high threat areas of NVN were to have two operational ECM pods (QRC 160-B/ALQ-71) on each aircraft. Prior to this, most reconnaissance sorties were supported either by pod-carrying escort aircraft, or were scheduled in conjunction with strike TOTs to benefit from the jamming coverage of strike aircraft pods and EB-66B electronic countermeasures. With the advent of their self-carried ECM capability, the RF-4Cs of the 432d TRW changed their tactics. Leaving the long-necessary low altitude ingress and pop-up, the photo reconnaissance pilots returned to the mid-altitude and high-altitude range, using the Radar Homing and Warning (RHAW) equipment to warn of SAM radar activity and launch, and the pods to provide noise jamming. To improve both ECM coverage and MIG protection, the two-ship formation was employed during daytime operation; during night runs the pilots retained the one-aircraft concept. 5/

The use of pods at night differed from that of the constant jamming, two-aircraft formation used in daylight operations. Without the covering effect of nearby strikes and ECM backup, most pilots preferred to ingress at low altitude, using terrain screening as much as possible and keeping the pods off. According to one RF-4C pilot, the night tactics (after discovery by enemy radar) contained real elements of finesse. He said:[6]

> *"Our pod procedure for night flying is the inverse of daytime procedures. We jam only if they come up on us and get serious, and then we leave the pods on for about ten seconds. While he (the NVN radar operator) is backing off on the gain, we drop some chaff, turn and descend from MEA (Minimum En route Altitude) to TFO (Terrain Following Override, using the forward-looking radar of the RF-4C). We then turn off the pods, which makes him have to turn up gain only to find a chaff blip--it says here. In any event it seems to work."*

Increased numbers integration and sophistication of the NVN radar net allowed the North Vietnamese to rely less and less heavily upon their Fan Song (SA-2 track-while-scan radar) and Firecan (AAA radar) equipment, against which the ECM pods were highly effective. Instead, the North Vietnamese used information from GCI and acquisition radar to plot an ingressing track force, and from there to pre-compute a point in space and the time the aircraft would be there. With this information, the SAMs could be launched without using the track-while-scan radar in its search mode, then acquired in flight with very little "on-air" time by the Fan Song. This gave hunter-killer aircraft (Wild Weasel/Iron Hand) insufficient time to suppress the site. In November 1967, a combat evaluation was initiated using the ALQ-71/QRC-160-8 pods to noise-jam the beacon receiver of the SA-2 missile, thus degrading missile

AIRCRAFT LOSS SUMMARY
1 July-31 December 1967

DTG	RP	UNIT	D/N	TARGET	ALT	SPD	HDG	ACFT	CALL SIGN	LOST TO
071705 Jul	SVN*	460TR	D	---	5M	---	---	RF101	Unk	Sus SA
270150 Jul	RPI*	460TR	N	Waterways	---	---	---	RF4C	Hipster	Unk
011221 Aug	RPVIA*	432TR	D	Storage Ar	18M	---	---	RF101	Eaglebeak 1	SAM
020324 Aug	RPIII*	432TR	D	LOCs	01H	---	---	RF4C	Baltic 1	SA
071521 Aug	SL*	432TR	D	En route	10M	310	---	RF4C	Edging	Unk
091552 Aug	RPI*	460TR	D	Tk Pk/RR	---	---	---	RF4C	Dispatch	Unk
09 Aug	SVN	460TR	D	---	---	---	---	RF101	Unk	Mid-air coll
121655 Aug	RPVIA*	432TR	D	JCS 13.00	18M	650	195	RF4C	Neptune 2	SAM
05 Sep	SVN	460TR	N	IR Recce	---	---	---	RF4C	Unk	Operational
121600 Sep	RPI*	432TR	D	LOCs	45H	---	360	RF4C	Slim	AW
161223 Sep	RPV*	432TR	D	RR Bridges	24M	---	200	RF101	Resale 2	MIG 21
161710 Sep	BR	432TR	D	En route	27M	---	190	RF101	Ace 1	Operational
170214 Sep	RPI*	460TR	N	POL Stores	---	---	300	RF4C	Nate 1	Unk
170956 Sep	RPVIA*	432TR	D	---	22M	720	128	RF4C	Kingdom 1	SAM
021443 Oct	RPIII	432TR	D	Airfield	22H	500	033	RF4C	Lotto 1	Operational
15 Oct	RPI*	460TR	N	IR Recon	---	---	---	RF4C	Unk	Unk
171635 Oct	Unk*	460TR	N	DMZ	---	---	---	RF4C	Kodak 64	Unk
181022 Oct	SL*	432TR	D	LOCs	54H	553	060	RF101	Goblin 1	AW
171148 Nov	RPVIA*	432TR	D	NE RR	24M	---	233	RF4C	Academic 1	SAM
171307 Nov	Thai	355TF	D	ELINT	---	---	---	EB66C	Elmo 1	Operational
191710 Nov	RPVIA*	432TR	D	---	15M	---	---	RF4C	Tile 1	SAM
201014 Nov	RPVIA*	432TR	D	Hanoi	---	---	210	RF4C	Damsel 2	85mm AAA
240154 Nov	RPVIA*	432TR	N	Wx Recon	---	---	---	RF4C	Shotgun	Unk
062145 Dec	Thai	355TF	N	ELINT	10H	---	---	EB66C	Sherwood 1	Operational

* Reported Combat Loss

FIGURE 2

tracking information. Combat evaluation of strike missions flown in the high threat SAM environment indicated this jamming was affecting SAM guidance, as miss distance by SA-2s showed a marked increase against aircraft equipped with the beacon jamming frequencies in the pod. On 14 December, the RF-4C aircraft began to add the beacon jamming capability on flights into the SAM ring. Although evaluation was not complete as of the end of Calendar Year 1967, the beacon jamming tactic appeared to have been highly successful in denying adequate tracking information to the SA-2. 7/

Reconnaissance Airframe Losses

The tactical reconnaissance force lost 24 aircraft during the six-month period, of which 18 were reported as combat losses. Sixteen RF-4Cs were lost, six RF-101s, and two EB-66s. The two EB-66Cs were operational losses following in-flight emergencies in Thailand, and resulted in the Dash ones being revised to reflect more accurate single engine performance data. NVN remained the highest threat area, accounting for 14 of the combat losses--five of these to SAMs in Route Package VI alone. Two aircraft were downed over Laos and one over South Vietnam from gunfire. The crew status and location of the 18th combat-attributed loss was unknown, but the intended target area was the western portion of the DMZ. 8/

In August and September, the highest losses of the period were registered. Five combat losses and one operational loss took place in August, with four combat and two operational losses recorded in September. Four combat losses were reported in November (two to SAMs in RP VIA), while no reconnaissance aircraft were downed by enemy fire in December. 9/ Figure 2 gives a

35

chronological loss summary from July through December.[10]

The 24 airframe losses brought the total USAF reconnaissance platforms lost during the war to 73 (not counting those of BLUE SPRING's drones or the high altitude SAC TROJAN HORSE programs).[11] The 24-lost figure nearly doubled that of the first six months of 1967 (14), and reflected an increased enemy ground fire base in NVN, along with an increase in operational losses; six versus the two recorded in the January-June period.[12]

Tactical Reconnaissance Sortie Accomplishment

The total tactical reconnaissance force (RF-4Cs, RF-101s, EB-66s, RB-57s, and EC-47s) flew 22,265 sorties during the period, a five percent decline from the first half of the year. By aircraft type, in- and out-country, statistics show that the RF-4Cs flew the largest portion of the reconnaissance effort:[13]

	RF-4C		RF-101		RB-57		EC-47		EB-66	
	IN	OUT	IN	OUT	IN	OUT	IN	OUT	IN	OUT
JUL	673	920	196	475	91	2	616	346	0	564
AUG	690	899	166	517	91	0	651	319	0	471
SEP	722	546	245	318	90	0	726	298	0	466
OCT	667	721	230	330	88	7	735	333	0	519
NOV	565	795	226	107	78	4	638	311	0	478
DEC	633	827	246	100	107	0	559	370	0	476
TOTAL	3,950	4,708	1,309	1,847	545	13	3,925	1,977	0	2,974

These figures were tabulated from monthly summaries; since they do not reflect updates, special missions, and adjustments in totals, etc., they will not correspond to year-end grand totals. They do, however, reflect significant trends in reconnaissance patterns, in-country and out-country. Photo reconnaissance in-country essentially paralleled efforts of the first half of the year for RF-4Cs, and RF-101s. Out-country, RF-101 photography declined by

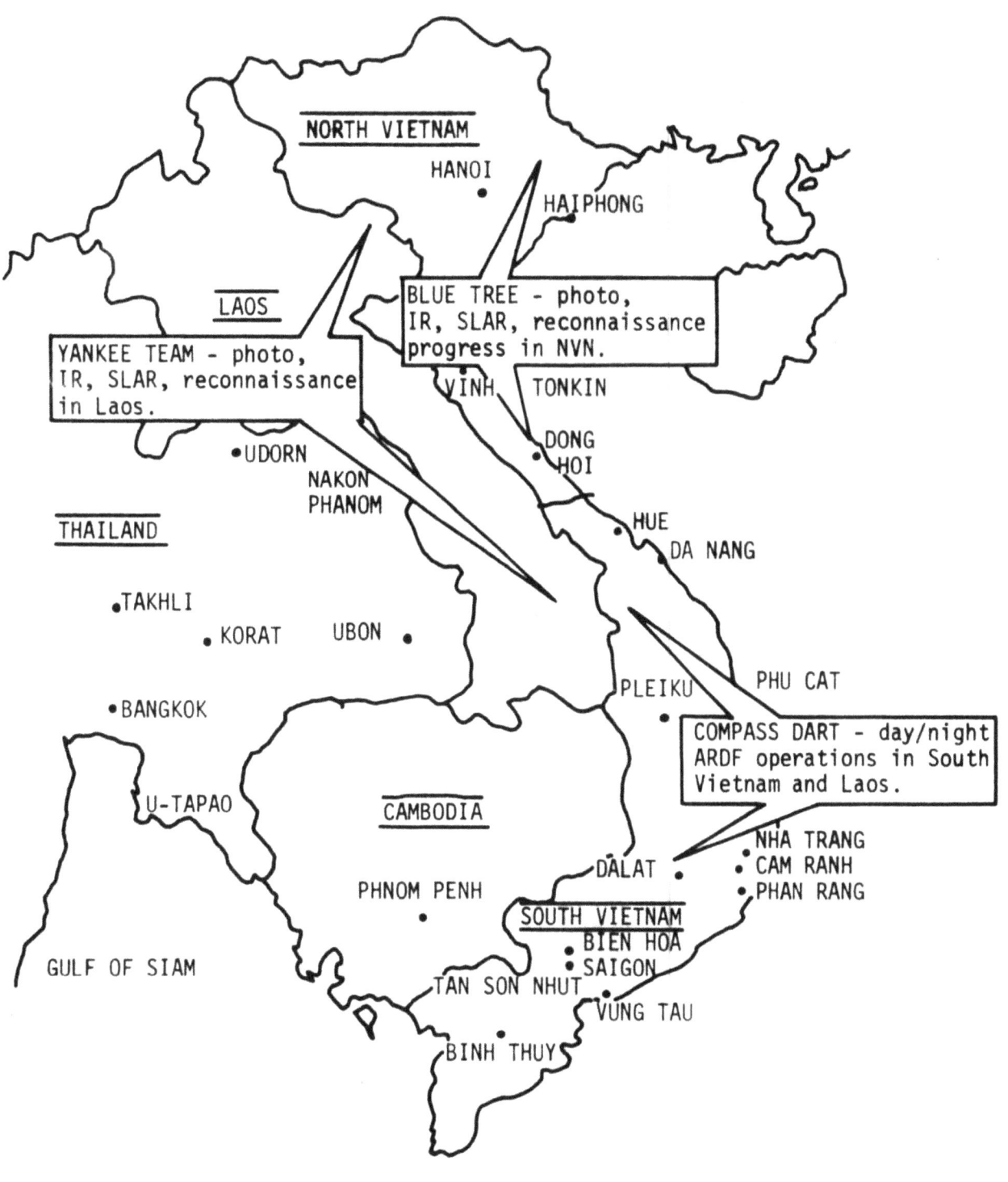

FIGURE 3

nearly 4,000 sorties and showed that--even prior to the redeployment of the 20th TRS resources from Udorn to Tan Son Nhut--there was concern for the aircraft's relative vulnerability when employed in high threat areas. EC-47 sorties (ARDF/COMPASS DART) showed a slight decrease in-country, but registered a 230 percent increase out-country; primarily in the southern sections of Laos. This indicated the attention being focused upon enemy communications as heavy infiltration became evident during the latter half of the year.

Significant codenamed reconnaissance programs with continuing operations in SEA included:

YANKEE TEAM (YT):	A CINCPAC-directed program of photographic reconnaissance against selected targets and LOCs in the BARREL ROLL, STEEL TIGER, and TIGER HOUND areas of Laos.
BLUE TREE (UE):	A program of photo reconnaissance against targets and LOCs in North Vietnam. USAF and USN aircraft are often fragged for UE/YT combined missions.
BLUE SPRINGS:	A CINCSAC-conducted drone aerial reconnaissance mission in SEA.
TROJAN HORSE:	Very high altitude operation of SAC U-2 aircraft to photograph selected targets and areas in SEA.
COMPASS DART:	ARDF-configured EC-47s principally engaged in intercepting, monitoring, and pinpointing enemy communications radio emissions in the low threat areas of SEA. (Fig. 3.)

The photo reconnaissance programs were tasked variously for area surveillance, route reconnaissance, point target reconnaissance, pre-strike and post-strike photography and occasional photo mapping of high-interest areas. Figures 4, 5, and 6 illustrate the versatility of the camera sensor system, showing, in turn, a medium-high altitude, high detail mosaic of the Kep (NVN) Airfield prior to runway extension; a low altitude post-strike picture of the Thai Nguyen Thermal Power Plant (NVN) showing extensive bomb damage from a previous strike; and a very low altitude (side looker) photo of an enemy AAA emplacement, catching the gunners completely unaware and with tarpaulins securely tied over their guns. 14/

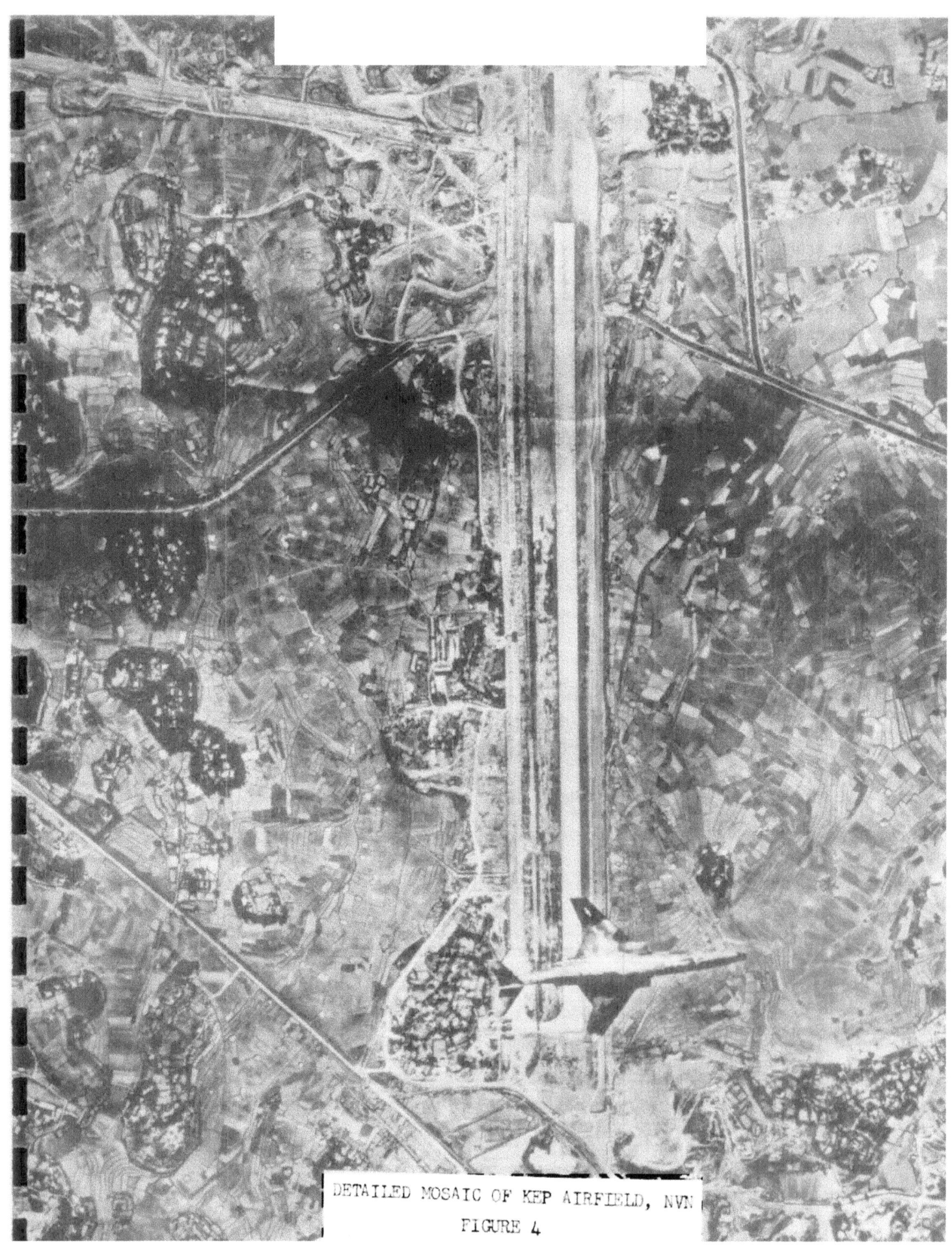

DETAILED MOSAIC OF KEP AIRFIELD, NVN
FIGURE 4

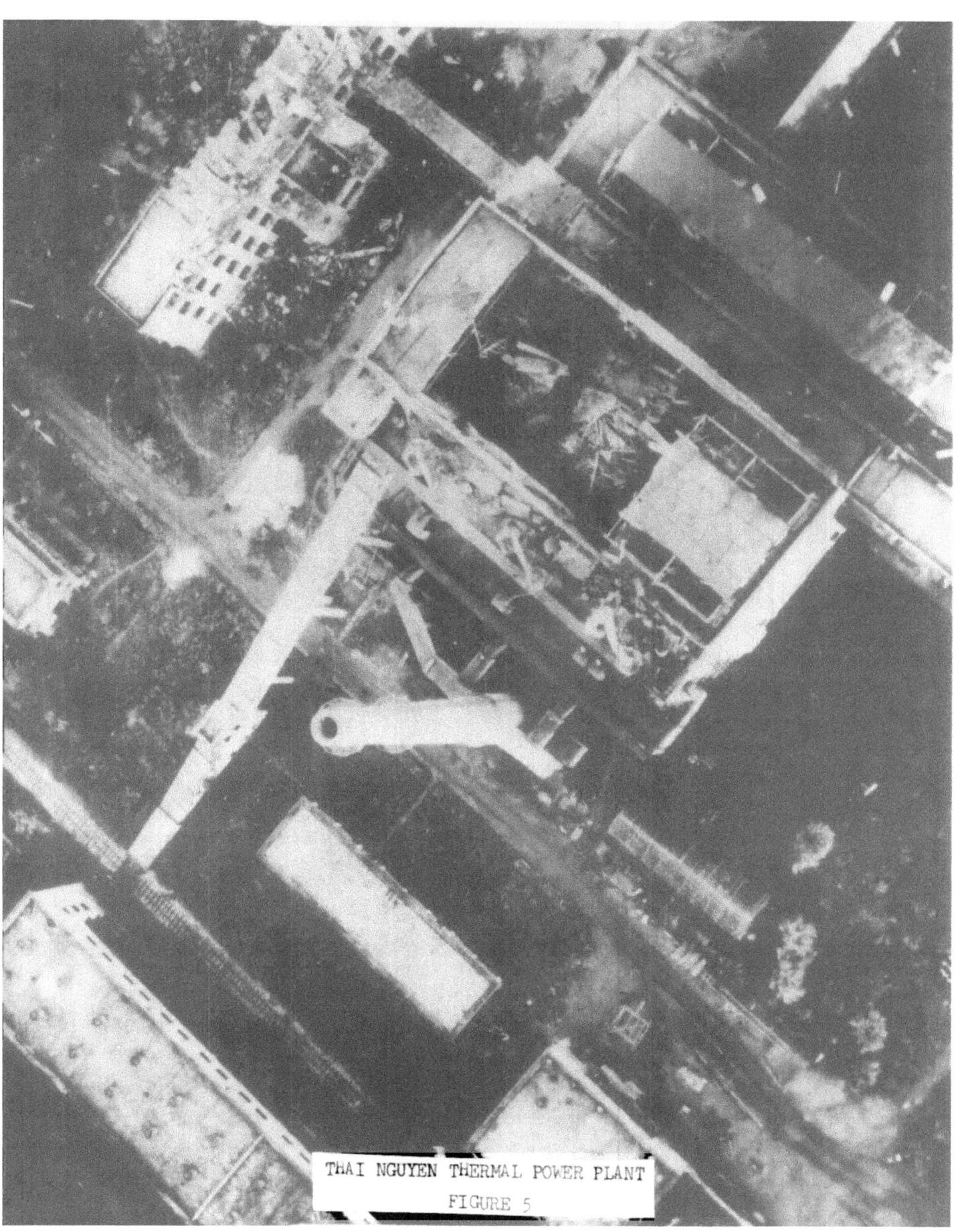

THAI NGUYEN THERMAL POWER PLANT
FIGURE 5

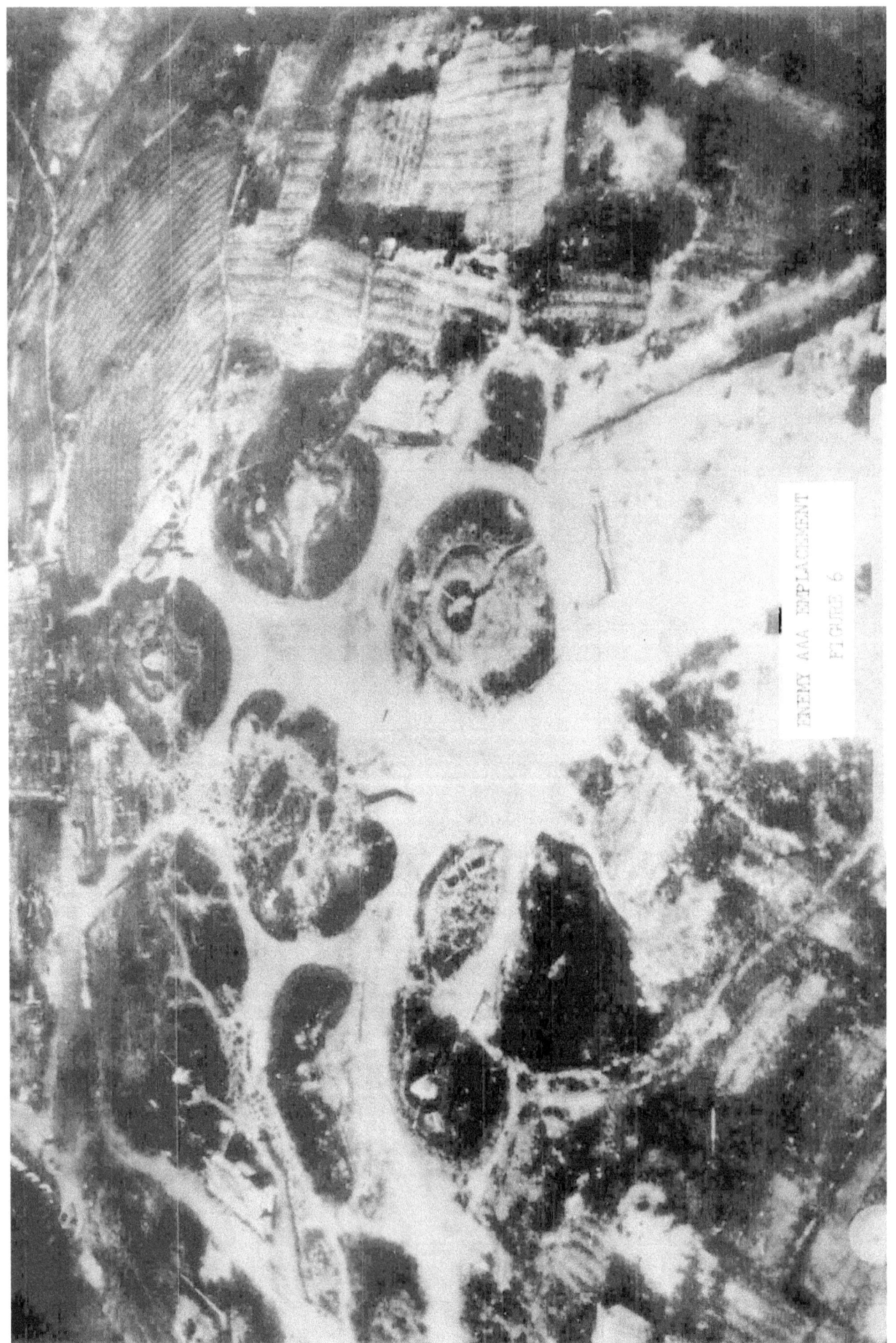

ENEMY AAA EMPLACEMENT
FIGURE 6

CHAPTER IV

ARC LIGHT PROGRAM

B-52 operations in Southeast Asia, known as the ARC LIGHT program, continued to assist in the defeat of the enemy through maximum destruction, disruption, and harassment of major command control centers, supply storage facilities, logistic systems, enemy troops, and lines of communication in selected target areas. The B-52 had the capability of carrying approximately 60,000 pounds of ordnance consisting of 500, 750, and 1,000-pound high explosive bombs, cluster bomb units, and munitions canisters containing anti-personnel bomblets. Thus it gave COMUSMACV the capability of delivering a mass saturation of bombs in a relatively large area with the size of the B-52 force being the only limitation. 1/

During the period July-December 1967, B-52s carried out a total of 4,969 sorties distributed as follows: 2/

	JUL	AUG	SEP	OCT	NOV	DEC
Total B-52 sorties	836	829	833	847	816	808
North Vietnam		117*	266	214	63	77
DMZ - South	30		226	141	45	72
DMZ - North			96	99	36	110
South Vietnam	600	596**	245	354	541	306
Laos	206	117	0	39	131	243

* Including DMZ North.
** Including DMZ South.

Appendix VI shows the number of B-52 sorties and tons of ordnance expended in support of major ground operations (three battalions or larger) during the second half of 1967.

Dak To

ARC LIGHT sorties, along with tactical air, supported U.S. and ARVN forces operating in the Dak To area in the fall of 1967. On 1 November, Allied forces began moving units into the area around Dak To, a small Vietnamese village in the central highlands province of Kontum in the II Corps Tactical Zone. Approximately five kilometers southwest of Dak To was an airfield with a 4,200-foot hard surface runway, which was flanked by U.S. forces and ARVN CIDG forces to the east and west. Elements of five enemy regiments numbering more than 10,000 NVA regulars were located nearby. At 1230 hours on 4 November, two companies of the U.S. 3d Battalion, 12th Infantry Brigade, made contact five kilometers south of Dak To, with an estimated enemy battalion. During the next two days, 74 tactical air sorties and 15 ARC LIGHT sorties were flown in the area as the enemy increased his pressure. For the next week and a half, heavy, sporadic engagements continued as friendly forces encountered enemy defensive positions in the rugged terrain. 3/

From 8 through 14 November, an additional 354 tactical air sorties were flown. B-52s flew 62 sorties and dropped more than 1,000 tons of HE ordnance on targets south-southwest of Dak To. On 15 November, the enemy succeeded in disrupting US/ARVN resupply efforts with mortar attacks on the Dak To Airfield. The following day the enemy mortared the CIDG Command Post at 1100 hours and overran a small village four kilometers south of Dak To. ARC LIGHT and tactical sorties supported Allied forces as the fighting ranged from hill to hill, southwest and west of Dak To, near principal logistic routes into SVN from Laos and Cambodia.[4]

A total of 257 B-52 sorties were flown in support of American units and 48 sorties in support of ARVN troops northeast of Dak To. In the target areas south and west of the major engagements, numerous secondary explosions occurred; also, fortifications and infiltration routes were harassed. ARC LIGHT strikes were especially effective in destroying enemy ammunition caches along remote ravines that could not be searched by ground troops.[5]

Operation NEUTRALIZE

In the fall of 1967, 7AF initiated Operation NEUTRALIZE for the purpose of finding the enemy artillery and storage areas in and near the DMZ, and attacking them with tactical air and B-52 strikes. The following paragraphs are limited to detailing some of the highlights of B-52 participation in this operation.[6]

As previously noted, the mission of Operation NEUTRALIZE was to reduce the enemy threat to the Dong Ha, Gia Linh, Camp Carrol, and Con Thien areas. The concept of operations was to bring massive, continuous airpower to bear on a relatively small area. Plans included two ARC LIGHT missions daily; one between 0500 and 0800 hours and another between 1100 and 1400 hours local. Each ARC LIGHT would be followed by approximately 36 tactical sorties. Additional sorties would continue to strike on 24-hour basis. Seventh Air Force was prepared to commit 65 tactical sorties per day to this operation beginning on 11 September and terminating with the start of the northeast monsoon or until the threat in the DMZ had been substantially neutralized. The 1st MAW was requested to provide 36 strike sorties per day. [7/]

On 9 September, 7AF requested MACV to obtain blanket approval for ARC LIGHT strikes in two sections of the NEUTRALIZE area. Within these sections, 7AF would have selected specific segments for attack based on intelligence collected by its Intelligence Task Force. Prior to strikes, 7AF would have determined that the targeted segments did not contain populated villages, shrines, temples, national monuments, friendly forces, and noncombatants. Under this plan, which was approved by CINCPAC, 7AF also advised MACV when each segment was selected for attack. The ARC LIGHT TOTs were coordinated with 7AF so that maximum tactical air follow-up could be provided. [8/]

From 11 September through 25 September, 7AF flew 403 strike sorties and 25 reconnaissance sorties. USMC supported with 309 strike sorties. Adverse weather resulted in 213 of these strikes being conducted by COMBAT SKYSPOT for which no visual results were available. A total of 311 ARC LIGHT sorties were flown in and near the DMZ. Results of these strikes were six occupied field artillery positions destroyed, one damaged; eight occupied AAA positions destroyed; 65 secondary explosions and fires. ARC LIGHT produced 28 secondary explosions for a total of 93; eight bunkers destroyed; three structures destroyed; four trucks destroyed and two damaged; and an estimated 95 enemy killed by air. [9/]

After the first weeks, the weather improved and the sortie rate against the enemy positions increased. By 4 October, 1,483 tactical airstrikes (791

AF, 649 USMC, and 43 USN) had been flown in the operation. Fifty-three ARC LIGHT missions, consisting of 496 sorties, had also dropped 12,525 tons of munitions in support of Operation NEUTRALIZE. Results of the ARC LIGHT missions included 174 secondary explosions observed by flight crews. [10/]

Enemy positions in the Operation NEUTRALIZE area were heavily defended by AAA. The presence of a continued SAM threat in the TALLY HO/DMZ area was was also verified by the firing of two SAMs at a three-ARC LIGHT formation on 17 September. From 1800 to 1805 hours, two EB-66Cs in the area intercepted Fan Song tracking and guidance signals, and issued SAM warnings. At 1805 hours, the flight of B-52s at 37,000 - 38,000 feet, was just south of the DMZ, inbound to a target north of the DMZ. The B-52s intercepted the tracking and guidance signals and, shortly thereafter, two SAMs detonated one-half and one and one-half nautical miles from the formation. Both evasive action and jamming were employed. No damage was sustained, and the aircraft proceeded to the alternate target. [11/]

Adverse weather and the lack of sufficient reconnaissance and ground follow-up made it difficult to accurately assess damage inflicted on enemy forces. However, the role played by airpower in lessening enemy pressure against Marine forward positions was reflected in significant decreases in enemy fire. For example, 6,100 incoming rounds were received in July, 51,100 in August, and 7,400 in September. This dropped to 3,600 rounds in October. COMUSMACV announced the siege at Con Thien was temporarily lifted, although intermittent enemy artillery fire was expected to continue. [12/]

Laos

In the Laos interdiction program, B-52s flew 206 sorties during July delivering 5,382 tons of ordnance principally along Routes 922 and 92. The 117 sorties flown in August were concentrated against validated truck parks, storage areas, covered bunkers, and fortified positions on routes in the east central panhandle area. The 3,214 tons of ordnance expended resulted in numerous secondary explosions reported by FACs performing visual reconnaissance on Routes 922, 23, and 92. During September, there were no B-52 sorties in Laos, as the ARC LIGHT effort was concentrated primarily against DMZ and NVN targets. In October, the B-52s expended 1,217 tons of ordnance in 39 sorties against targets along Route 12 south of Mu Gia Pass and Routes 922 and 110 near the Laotian/RVN border. The number of sorties rose to 131 in November, and strikes were directed primarily against transshipment points, storage areas, and truck parks near Mu Gia Pass. The 243 ARC LIGHT sorties flown in Laos during December were an 85 percent increase as compared to the November total of 131. The 7,324 tons of ordnance were expended primarily in the Mu Gia Pass area, Cambodia-Laos-RVN tri-border region, and along Routes 92, 922, and 923. [13/]

Restrictions

At midyear, efforts were underway to remove the ARC LIGHT restrictions, which were hampering operational efficiency. These restrictions prohibited B-52 strikes in Laos by Thailand-based B-52s; limited B-52 strikes in Laos from Guam-based aircraft to hours of darkness; and prohibited over-flights of Laos by B-52s en route to targets in North or South Vietnam. The B-52s were originally deployed to U-Tapao for reasons of economy and timeliness of response; however, the Laos overflight restriction negated these advantages. Reaction time to Laotian targets could be as little as four hours and twenty minutes compared with nine hours by Andersen-based aircraft. Actual mission flight time to the target could be reduced by four and one-half hours, if U-Tapao-based aircraft were allowed to overfly Laos en route to targets in Vietnam. 14/

B-52s flying the southern route around Cambodia and striking targets near 16 degrees latitude required approximately twice the number of flying hours required for the most direct route across Laos. Approximately $1.5 million in direct cost savings per month could be realized by overflying Laos. 15/

Another argument in favor of removing this restriction was that targets located in the vicinity of the DMZ, within possible SAM lethal radius, required some Laos overflight for SAM evasive maneuvers, preplanned diversion routing and altitude time separation. In many cases, target boxes located near the Laotian border had to be oriented in an undesirable position to preclude or minimize daylight overflight of Laos. Security of the B-52 force was jeopardized by the restriction and the resultant requirement to schedule night TOTs, which reduced the effectiveness of the TINY TIM support. 16/

Also, limiting strikes of Guam B-52s in Laos to hours of darkness was considered tactically unsound. Maximum freedom was required to schedule strikes so that advantage could be taken of a divert situation for a target of opportunity in South Vietnam. 17/

In August, the American Ambassador in Vientiane agreed to recommend to the Secretary of State that current restrictions on use of U-Tapao-based

B-52 aircraft for ARC LIGHT strikes in Laos be lifted. However, this change would not alter requirements for cover strikes, for daylight restrictions, and for using approach routes south of Cambodia. The Ambassador stated that the question of the approach route north of Cambodia and of overflying Laotian territory by B-52 aircraft had international ramifications. While some eventual change in the flight pattern in the future was not ruled out, the Ambassador did not think this was the appropriate time to bring the issue up with Thai officials.[18/]

On 29 November, the Secretary of State informed the American Embassy, Vientiane, that since B-52 operations from U-Tapao were now well established, it had been decided to authorize B-52 flights across Laos to targets in South Vietnam, North Vietnam, and northern South Vietnam. This action would enable improved ARC LIGHT response to urgent tactical requirements, such as in the Dak To and DMZ areas. Strikes against targets in southern South Vietnam would continue to be routed south of Cambodia. Both day and night strikes in Laos were authorized to increase flexibility necessary for optimum force utilization. The requirement for cover strikes in nearby South Vietnam was originally established to avoid acknowledging that strikes were being conducted against targets in Laos. But, since three to five ARC LIGHT missions were flown in Vietnam daily, providing adequate cover for normal operations, it was decided that cover strikes were no longer necessary. Accordingly, the Secretary of State informed the American Embassy at Vientiane that restrictions on overflight and daylight bombing, and requirements for cover strikes in South Vietnam were discontinued effective at 2400 hours on 5 December 1967.

The American Embassy, Bangkok, was successful in getting Thai concurrence in ARC LIGHT overflights of Laos, subject to minor stipulations and conditions which did not substantially affect operational efficiency.[19]

Increased Sortie Effort

Efforts were also made during this period to increase the B-52 sortie rate from 800 to 1,200 per month. COMUSMACV forwarded a request to CINCPAC in September 1967, stating that approximately 40 sorties per day were required rather than the present 27. The increase was needed to keep pressure on the enemy's supply and infiltration system, while at the same time thwarting his efforts to mass along the DMZ and western borders. During September alone, an average of 24 sorties per day were scheduled for the DMZ area. This concentration of the B-52 effort along the DMZ had been possible, because of the lack of significant enemy activity in other parts of SVN and the poor weather conditions in Laos. With the reopening of routes in Laos, however, and the enemy buildup in other areas, the number of B-52 targets increased and required a corresponding increase in the number of sorties.[20]

COMUSMACV further stated that although bomb damage assessment was difficult to obtain, a total of 3,665 confirmed, estimated, and unconfirmed enemy personnel were KIA by B-52 strikes during 1966-1967. That total did not include an estimated 3,000 casualties caused by the combination of artillery, tactical air and B-52 strikes in the DMZ. Collateral sources revealed that B-52 strikes were causing increasing damage. Heavy aerial bombardment had apparently caused a change in the enemy's pattern of operations and movements, and more of his efforts were defensive. Consequently, it was increasingly difficult for him to initiate large-scale activities.[21]

Recent experience in the DMZ area pointed up the requirement for maximum concentration of B-52 strikes against areas of enemy concentration of troops and weapons. During the 69-day period from 17 August to 24 October 1967, an average of 24 sorties per day was scheduled in the DMZ area. The capability to deliver approximately 40 sorties per day would have enabled the U.S. to keep the pressure on the enemy throughout his supply and infiltration system, while pounding away at the DMZ and western borders.[22]

In support of his request to JCS for increased ARC LIGHT sorties, CINCPAC pointed out that the concentrated B-52 pressure against DMZ targets had been a major contributing factor in denying success to the enemy in that area. Continuing enemy activity in the DMZ and major supply concentrations near the Mu Gia Pass in Laos provided targets that should have been struck on a continuing basis. However, the diversion of major portions of available ARC LIGHT capability to high threat areas necessitated reduced bombing effect against other important targets.[23]

JCS responded in October that, for the present, the normal ARC LIGHT sortie rate was to remain at the 800 level, with sufficient forces deployed to insure a capability for a rapid increase in ARC LIGHT sorties to as many as 1,200 per month when the situation warranted it. JCS requested that approval be obtained from the Royal Thai Government (RTG) to increase the number of B-52s based at U-Tapao from 15 to 30 aircraft.[24]

In November, the Secretary of State requested the American Ambassador in Thailand to approach the RTG to obtain permission for augmentation of the B-52 force at U-Tapao. At the end of November, the RTG approved an increase in the B-52 force at U-Tapao by ten aircraft, giving the force a total strength of 24 aircraft and 1,000 personnel.[25/]

In December, CSAF informed CINCPAC and CINCSAC of his program to increase the ARC LIGHT sortie rate from 800 to 1,200 by 1 February 1968. Due to programmed rotation of forces on Guam and current repair/construction work at U-Tapao, the increase in forces was to be delayed until January 1968. The proposed force basing to support the new sortie rate was as follows:[26/]

	ARC LIGHT	
	B-52	KC-135
ANDERSEN	59	2
U-TAPAO	20	0
KADENA	0	33
CHING CHUAN KANG, TAIWAN	0	35
	79	70

Funding had been requested for construction of additional B-52 facilities at U-Tapao. Final beddown was to be made in June 1968 with basing and forces as indicated below:[27/]

	ARC LIGHT	
	B-52	KC-135
ANDERSEN	47	2
U-TAPAO	25	0
KADENA	0	25
CHING CHUAN KANG, TAIWAN	0	0
	72	27

The manpower spaces required by 1 February 1968 were 2,677. The end position manpower spaces required to sustain the 1,200 sortie rate were to decrease to 2,313. Of the 1,016 PCS authorizations required, 610 were to be for SAC and 506 for PACAF. The remaining 1,297 spaces were to be provided by SAC on a TDY basis. Increased manpower spaces for FY-69 to add 56 officers, 873 airmen, and 87 civilians were requested. The combined additive personnel programmed into Thailand was not to exceed 1,000, as approved by the Secretary of Defense. [28/]

Funds in the amount of $10 million for the additional construction at U-Tapao AB to support the permanent basing of ten additional B-52s were requested from the OSD contingency fund for SEA. Total construction funding for the additional B-52 facilities at U-Tapao was to be approximately $9.96 million. [29/]

Bomb Damage Assessment

Bomb damage assessment (BDA) for B-52 strikes had been a problem since the inception of the ARC LIGHT program. The enemy's policy of policing the bombed area, the delay in ground follow-up, and the dense canopy over much of the area prevented an accurate body count. During the period of 18 June 1966-31 October 1967, there were 1,350 missions flown in North and South Vietnam, totaling 9,680 sorties. BDA was obtained on 801 of the 1,350 missions and included SAC crew reports, 308 photo interpretation reports, 286 VR, 317 ground follow-ups, and 13 detailed helicopter reconnaissance missions. The results showed 2,497 KIA, 313 WIA, and 1,953 secondary explosions. In addition, BDA reported the following: [30/]

	Destroyed	Damaged	Undamaged
Weapons Positions	105	293	927
Structures/Fortifications/Storage Areas	4,338	3,065	8,655
Modes of Transportation	272	39	342
Bases/Camps	39	18	88

COMUSMACV noted that the terrain, type of fortifications, and timeliness of coverage did not provide ideal circumstances for photographic exploitation, and that, in general, BDA by means of photography appeared to be of little value in this area. To improve post-strike photographic reconnaissance coverage of ARC LIGHT strikes, COMUSMACV recommended employing a selective tasking based upon analysis of the target area prior to strike. Pre-strike photography, canopy coverage, intelligence, command interest, and time of strike were to be considered. If photographic exploitation appeared likely, a high priority reconnaissance tasking would have improved the timeliness of coverage and substantially increased the overall value of the post-strike program. 31/

With respect to ARC LIGHT effectiveness, the CG III MAF stated that he had made limited use of B-52 preparatory strikes in support of ground operations. However, he had used ARC LIGHT strikes extensively at Khe Sanh in late April, early May, and from mid-June to November in the eastern DMZ area. He stated that ARC LIGHT strikes had proved particularly effective in the attack on known troop concentrations and hard targets (fortifications, supply/storage areas, artillery/mortar/rocket positions, and communications/supply routes). The concentration of ARC LIGHT strikes in the DMZ area had apparently inflicted heavy casualties and destroyed supplies and equipment. In addition, the strikes had forced the enemy to change his tactics; i.e., he now dispersed his artillery and if he concentrated his forces at all, he attempted to do so within three kilometers of friendly forces. The enemy's supplies and storage areas had decreased and had been relocated further from his operating forces. Many of his defensive positions had been destroyed and no longer served as a haven. ARC LIGHT strikes could effectively counter a buildup of long duration in a relatively large area. They were successful in at least temporarily dislodging the enemy from assembly areas just south of the DMZ, and in the vicinity of Con Thien and in the destruction of his prepositioned supplies. However, the CG, III MAF, pointed out that in a spoiling attack wherein forces had to respond rapidly against an enemy discovered in an attack position in proximity to friendly forces, B-52 effectiveness was derogated by the time involved between request and execution, and the safety zone restrictions. Due to the time required to effect clearance requirements and the delay after clearance had been effected, the enemy frequently had left the target area before TOT. [32/]

The enemy had been forced to divert personnel from offensive to defensive activities and afford high priority to camouflage efforts. A captured document revealed that dummy troop locations were to be constructed to deceive reconnaissance aircraft. Other documents gave directions for building breastworks and shelters which would afford protection from B-52s. An NVA prisoner stated that his unit's first action on arriving at a campsite was to dig holes for protection against airstrikes. He also reported that certain soldiers were assigned solely to watching aircraft, while others concentrated on ground fighting. [33/]

Interdiction

A major objective of the ARC LIGHT program was the destruction of material being infiltrated into South Vietnam. An analysis of strikes during the first eight months of 1967 indicated a significant increase in reported secondary explosions from target areas located along infiltration routes. There were also other indications supporting the effectiveness of the interdiction program on the enemy's logistical system. His decision to operate directly through the DMZ was undoubtedly influenced by logistical considerations. The enemy also had taken high risks in unsuccessful attempts to supply arms and ammunition to coastal areas by large trawlers. [34/]

Psychological Effect

Reports indicated that the psychological effects suffered by the victims of B-52 strikes were a major factor in the overall effectiveness of the ARC LIGHT program. The noise, shock, and destruction of the B-52s produced an intense fear among the enemy, accompanied by a sense of helplessness and isolation. Even individuals not directly injured by the blast might suffer secondary effects such as temporary deafness or pains in the chest. The fear and doubt among the victims of a B-52 strike often remained long after the strike. US/GVN forces attempted to exploit these fears and misgivings through psychological operations. Large quantities of leaflets which described the B-52 and its powerful bombs were dropped into the area after a strike. The pamphlets urged VC/NVA to defect and encouraged civilians to flee to the safety and security of government-controlled areas. [35/]

CHAPTER V

AIRLIFT

Organization

Airlift resources in the second half of 1967 retained the basic organizational structure and the command and control channels of the preceding six months, although some minor changes were promulgated. The 315th Air Commando Wing (C-123s), the 483d Tactical Airlift Wing (C-7s), and the 2d Aerial Port Group remained stationed in-country and assigned to the 834th Air Division. C-130 resources continued to be provided from 315th Air Division resources on a shuttle basis from off-shore facilities.

Two minor changes in nomenclature were made to more accurately reflect the combat nature of the airlift. In recognition of its combat function, the C-123 wing and squadrons on 1 August had "Troop Carrier" added to their unit designations. At the same time, the C-7 wing and squadrons were redesignated from "Troop Carrier" to "Tactical Airlift". [1]

Somewhat more substantive was the organization of Detachments 1 and 2 of the 834th Air Division at Tan Son Nhut AB and Cam Ranh Bay AB, respectively. These detachments replaced 315th Air Division Operating Locations "AB" at Tan Son Nhut and "AC" at Cam Ranh Bay, and had 36 PCS personnel assigned to each detachment. Since 1965, the question of an in-country C-130 wing had been seriously considered, but rejected. The 315th Air Division continued to provide a designated number of operationally ready airframes, flying them out of South Vietnam to the offshore bases whenever maintenance was required. [2]

Maintenance was the crux of the matter in view of the advocates of an in-country wing. Considerable time and manpower were lost from such a shuttle system, and in-country maaintenance was inevitably required from resources programmed for other aircraft and units. Thus, the organization of Dets 1 and 2 was a step toward bringing maintenance and operational control of C-130s in-country. However, the maintenance program was initially staffed with 500 TDY personnel from various PACAF numbered air forces. According to the Commander, 834th Air Division, the detachments were still not the full answer:[3/]

> *"From a management standpoint, this organizational arrangement has proven to be less than desirable. The flying hours of these two detachments are equivalent to the hours normally flown by two C-130A/B wings. The short sortie lengths, high gross weight takeoffs, and combat conditions found in the in-country operation impose extraordinary demands on aircrews and maintenance personnel. The maintenance task is being accomplished with a cross-section of transient airmen grades and skills from units not enjoying the Southeast Asia manning considerations. The lack of a stabilized working force hinders managers and supervisors in identifying qualified personnel and in developing the espirit-de-corps in this combat environment.*
>
> *"The question of placing a C-130 wing in-country should be reconsidered. From an airlift manager's standpoint, this would be the least acceptable action that would produce the results desired. The SEA/PACOM C-130 Airlift Study, finalized last March (1967), clearly indicated that a PCS wing in-country would provide the most efficient use of C-130 resources."*

Another aspect of a Single Manager concept concerned the respective merits of common user versus a dedicated user system. When the C-7 Caribou had been transferred from the Army to the Air Force on 1 January 1967, it had been assigned as a dedicated user to the Army and remained so through 1967. The

834th Air Division Commander, in his November 1967 End of Tour Report, cautioned against an attempt to integrate the C-7s into the common service airlift system: 4/

> *"Total integration of C-7A operation into the SEA Common Service Airlift System and elimination of dedicated user support in order to achieve maximum utilization of all airlift resources is a tempting move on the surface. Experience indicates that the ground forces have a valid need for unscheduled incidental airlift support, similar to that provided by Air Force base support aircraft. With an aircraft such as the C-7A, the Air Force has proven that it can and will provide such support to ground forces. Enthusiasm for eliminating dedicated user support should be tempered by the thought that the need is valid and must be filled by the Air Force or by ground force organic aircraft. The latter solution certainly would not advance any Air Force cause."*

Redeployments

During the last half of 1967, the twin problems of airfield congestion and mortar attacks had an adverse effect on the airlift system. The threat of rocket and mortar attacks had increased steadily during the year, compounding the vulnerability of congested bases such as Da Nang and Tan Son Nhut. As a result, aircraft permanently in-country were moved to less exposed or less crowded bases. For instance, in the last quarter of 1967, the C-7s stationed at Can Tho were returned to Vung Tau, while those at Nha Trang and Pleiku were moved back to Cam Ranh Bay. This was done to provide better maintenance and more physical security. 5/

On 15 June, the 315th Air Commando Wing and one squadron at Tan Son Nhut moved to Phan Rang, a base off the beaten cargo track. Some C-123s remained at Da Nang as an operating location. This move to Phan Rang reduced congestion at the three older bases (built in French colonial days), but placed C-123 operations away from the major cargo generation points. According to the Commander, 834th Air Division, studies indicated that 24 percent of all initial sorties from Phan Rang were flown by empty aircraft.[6/] The wing calculated that being stationed at Phan Rang cost perhaps 1,800 tons per month.[7/]

The enemy mortar threat to air bases was a very real one. On 15 July, eleven aircraft were destroyed at Da Nang in a mortar attack, including six F-4s and two C-130s.[8/] In September, this threat brought about the redeployment of C-123s from Da Nang to Phu Cat and Phan Rang. The move was termed temporary until revetments could be built at Da Nang. The effect of this move was a reduction by 85 tons per day during September in the C-123 operations in I Corps. Further, the air division commander estimated that the redeployment of the C-123 wing to Phan Rang and the pullback from Da Nang were the major causes for the 13 percent loss in C-123 tonnage in September.[9/]

Tonnage

Total tonnage moved for the six months increased from 102,900 tons in July to 111,836 tons in December. The increase in monthly C-130 tonnage (up from 58,800 tons to 71,300 tons) was offset by declines in the tonnage moved by C-7s (down from 19,600 to 18,100) and C-123s (down from 19,600 to 18,100). Cumulative statistics for July through December were as follows:[10/]

	Avg Acft Assigned	Total Sorties	Total Passengers	Total Cargo Tons	Total Tons
A-4 (RAAF)	6	4,536	34,212	1,684	5,789
C-7	90	78,610	532,557	49,291	113,198
C-123	62	46,557	414,915	78,926	128,734
C-130	57	64,444	850,149	292,357	394,374
TOTAL	215	194,147	1,831,833	422,258	642,095

Of special interest was evaluation of the C-7 program at the completion of its first year under Air Force management. The improvement justified the Air Force assumption of management. The operationally ready rate rose from 65 to 77 percent. When the Air Force received the C-7, a goal of 19,000 tons to be moved per month was established for the end of the year. While it was surpassed in March, tonnage by December was down to 18,100. Initially, the wing flew 2.5 hours per aircraft per day, but that was raised to 3.0.[11/] The cumulative statistics comparing the Army and Air Force were as follows:[12/]

	US Army 1966 Avg	Dec 1966	USAF 1967 Avg	Dec 1967
Flying Hours	6,962	6,451	8,322	8,818
Sorties Flown	10,405	9,499	12,998	12,668
Total Tons	15,194	13,092	18,716	18,105
PAX Airlifted	67,097	60,843	85,600	85,016
Assigned Acft	96	95	90	90

Tactical Airlift

During the six-month period the airlift moved 642,000 tons, most of it in routine shipments. However, several large battles and operations did generate emergency requirements. The number of emergency sorties compared to total common service airlift sorties was 4.4 percent in July and rose steadily to 13.3 percent in November, the month of the battles of Loc Ninh and Dak To. The monthly average was 8.5 percent. In six months, the airlift flew 8,438 emergency sorties, including 255 tactical emergency (the highest priority) and 510 emergency resupply sorties.[13]

The major tactical airlift support during the period went to III MAF in Project 972--5,219 tons--(I Corps); to the 101st Airborne Division in Operation KLAMATH FALLS--9,273 tons--and to the 4th Infantry Division in MACARTHUR--7,882 tons--(both in II Corps), and to the 1st Infantry Division in SHENANDOAH II--7,892 tons--(III Corps).[14]

Total cargo aircraft losses for the six months were four C-7s, three C-123s, and five C-130s.[15] At Dak To, on the morning of 15 November, four C-130s were on the airstrip during a mortar attack of such precision that two were destroyed. The ammunition supply point also took several hits and was destroyed, necessitating a large aerial resupply the following week. However, to prevent a recurrence of the 15 November losses, only one C-130 was allowed on the ground at any one time.[16]

Technology

Technical developments concerned the C-123K jet pods, the use of the C-130 main fuel tank to transport POL, and combat use of the Parachute Low Altitude Delivery System (PLADS) and Low Altitude Parachute Extraction System (LAPES) aerial bulk resupply systems. The first C-123K model had been delivered in-country on 1 May 1967, and through the last half of the year the program was in full production. It was estimated that the modification program would be completed in the spring of 1968.[17/] The jet pods allowed the K model to climb at approximately 1,000 feet per minute with one engine shut down versus the B model's ability to climb at 100 feet per minute or less. Also, the K model could carry 2,000 pounds more allowable cabin load.

Experience, according to the 834th Commander, had also shown that the jets were used much more than originally planned:[18/]

> "A number of these aircraft have been operated in-country for several months and we have a fair experience based on them. For instance, it was originally thought that the jet engines would need to be operated only ten percent of the time the recips are operated as they are used for take-off, climb, descent, and landing. However, due to the short sortie lengths found in Vietnam, experience shows us that upwards of 40 percent of the time the jets are used. In addition, it has been decided to use the jets during airdrop missions as an increased safety factor and because they present a more stable platform. For planning purposes, the overall use of the jets will equate to approximately 60 percent of the flying hour program. This usage far exceeds that originally planned. The effects will be keenly felt in spare part support, engine life, and maintenance."

In October, the air division began experiementing with delivering 7,000 gallons of fuel per sortie using the C-130 main fuel tank. In comparison with the bladder delivery system, use of the fuel tanks moved 2,000 gallons more per sortie and also eliminated the need to return empty bladder bags, thus freeing cargo space.[19/]

Work also went on concerning LAPES and PLADS. The Commander, 834th Air

LOW ALTITUDE PARACHUTE EXTRACTION SYSTEM

FIGURE 7

Division, did not consider there was much need for PLADS, since increased accuracy in the Container Delivery System would adequately meet requirements. However, LAPES, with its ability to release pallatized cargo a few feet off the airstrip, had its use where pinpoint accuracy was desired (Fig. 7). LAPES was used to successfully resupply both Bu Dop, in III Corps, and Khe Sanh, in I Corps.[20/]

CHAPTER VI

HERBICIDE OPERATIONS

The marked increase in targeting requirements, operational commitments, and herbicide production and delivery, presented additional problems in the execution of the herbicide mission. Operational commitments had increased sortie rates from 315 in October 1966, to 468 in June 1967, and in II Corps alone, targets had increased to more than 1,800.[1/]

Reduced Sorties

Initial programming of herbicide delivery was based on an assumed delivery capability of 1.33 sorties per assigned aircraft per day. Requirements were based on 18 aircraft (minus one aircraft used for the mosquito control mission). The 1.33 sortie rate apparently did not take into consideration weather, maintenance, and battle damage. In October 1966, Seventh Air Force informed MACV that it had the capability to carry out only 1.2 sorties per aircraft. The reduction to 1.2 sorties was acceptable to MACV, since the herbicide available after the basic sortie rate had been flown by Ranch Hand aircraft could be used in the helicopter spray system. However, MACV did not believe it advisable to reduce the Ranch Hand commitment below this programmed level, because of requests from tactical commanders for more defoliation and crop destruction support.[2/]

As the sortie rate began to drop off in the spring and summer of 1967, 7AF advised MACV on 13 July of further reduction in its sortie rate capability. New empirical data revealed that Ranch Hand operations were able to support a sortie rate of only 1.0 per day per possessed aircraft. 7AF felt that MACV should give consideration to ordering herbicide on this basis. MACV recommended that if 7AF could not improve the 1.0 rate by any other means, it should utilize enough additional aircraft in the Ranch Hand operation to produce 612 sorties per month for FY68, and 864 sorties per month for FY69 and beyond.[3/]

COMUSMACV informed CINCPAC on 24 July, that primarily the 1.33 sortie rate had not been maintained, because of weather conditions and the fact that many priority targets required long flying times from the C-123 operating bases. Several high priority targets, however, had been developed near the base of C-123 operations; the feasibility of herbicide reloading points in the II CTZ was being investigated; and the C-123K model aircraft had been requested. COMUSMACV believed these factors would assist in achieving and maintaining a sortie rate of 1.2 per assigned aircraft for a total of 612 sorties per month for the remainder of FY68. FY69 requirements were computed on the same sortie rate for 24 C-123 aircraft.[4/]

Additionally, eight AGAVENCO spray systems to be used in UH-1D helicopters had been ordered in May 1967. The herbicide capacity of this system was 200 gallons, and it was estimated that each unit could fly two sorties per day, a total of 3,200 gallons of herbicide per day. Based on these considerations, COMUSMACV computed that the total requirements for all types of herbicide for FY68 was 8,856,000 gallons, with the following average monthly breakdown:[5/]

```
17 C-123 aircraft at 1.2 sorties per day per aircraft ...... 612,000 gals
 8 AGAVENCO spray systems at 2 sorties per day ............  96,000 gals
Ground-based spray .......................................  30,000 gals
    Total per month                                        738,000 gals
```

he total requirement for FY69 was 11,880,000 gallons of all types of herbicide, ith the average monthly herbicide requirement as follows:

```
24 C-123 aircraft at 1.2 sorties per day per aircraft ...... 864,000 gals
 8 AGAVENCO spray systems at 2 sorties per day ............  96,000 gals
Ground-based spray .......................................  30,000 gals
    Total per month                                        990,000 gals
```

7AF suggested that MACV requirements, as outlined here, should be reassessed in light of maximum delivery capability, rather than desired support of field commanders, to preclude stockpiling of herbicide beyond foreseeable delivery potential. 7AF felt that procurement should be in consonance with delivery capacity which, in turn, would lessen the impact upon production facilities and the civilian market. [6/]

Both JCS and CSAF had expressed concern with the underconsumption of herbicide and the impact on procurement. JCS pointed out that, except for May and June 1967, the actual expenditures of herbicide were considerably below allocated quantities. This low expenditure rate made it difficult to justify the continued total preemption by the military, of herbicide normally available for U.S. civilian use. CSAF informed CINCPACAF, in October, that he had temporarily delayed contract proceedings with industry for procurement of FY69 herbicides, until resolution of the actual 1.0 sortie rate versus the MACV-programmed 1.2 sortie rate. [7/]

Based on empirical data from November 1966 to August 1967, 7AF reported that Ranch Hand operations showed an overall average of .993 sorties per day per possessed aircraft. During this period, there were only five months when the sortie rate was 1.0 or better. Weather was a major factor in sortie cancellations. In addition to inclement weather, which forced missions to abort, effective defoliation operations required a temperature of 85°F and wind velocity of ten knots or less. This requirement normally limited operations to morning hours. The average amount of herbicide delivered per sortie was 941 gallons. With 17 aircraft possessed and a maximum capability of 1.0 sorties per day per aircraft, the average 7AF capability was 476,550 gallons per month. Upon delivery of seven additional aircraft in FY68, this capability should increase to 672,777 gallons per month. For FY69 and FY70, 7AF capability would fall short of MACV requirement of 864,000 gallons per month by 191,223 gallons. To increase capability to stated requirements would require eight additional aircraft. [8]

COMUSMACV requested 7AF confirmation of the expected sortie production capability indicated here, prior to taking action to adjust its herbicide requirement. MACV used 1,000 gallons of herbicide per sortie as a planning figure to account for emergency dumps, spillage, and other shortages experienced during handling. Therefore, a capability of 714 sorties per month resulted in a planned herbicide expenditure rate of 714,000 gallons per month or 150,000 gallons less than the MACV requirement of 864,000 gallons per month. [9]

On 25 December, COMUSMACV informed CINCPAC that, after one year's

65

operation with 17 aircraft, 7AF had concluded that it could not maintain the 1.2 sortie rate, which had been the basis for computing MACV requirements in July 1967. 7AF had determined that 17 aircraft could average 506 sorties per month and that 24 aircraft could average 714 sorties per month. In addition to the seven aircraft programmed for FY69, 7AF requested eight additional aircraft to meet MACV requirements, but there were no indications that these aircraft would be made available. [10/]

Revised Estimate

COMUSMACV stated that the revised herbicide requirement for the second half of FY68 equaled 3,792,000 gallons based on the following average monthly breakdown: [11/]

```
17 C-123 aircraft at 506 sorties per month ............... 506,000 gals
 8 AGAVENCO spray systems at 2 sorties per day ...........  96,000 gals
Ground-based spray .......................................  30,000 gals
      Total per month                                      632,000 gals
```

The total requirement for FY69, including the seven aircraft already approved, was 10,080,000 gallons of all types of herbicide, based on the following average monthly breakdown:

```
24 C-123 aircraft at 714 sorties per month ............... 714,000 gals
 8 AGAVENCO spray systems at 2 sorties per day ...........  96,000 gals
Ground-based spray .......................................  30,000 gals
      Total per month                                      840,000 gals
```

Herbicide operations were planned for FY70 and beyond at the FY69 level.

Organization

The herbicide mission was the responsibility of the 12th Air Commando

Squadron, which was assigned for command and administrative control to the 315th ACW of the 834th AD. Operational control was exercised by 7AF through the Tactical Air Control Center (TACC). Manning consisted of 65 officers and 27 airmen for flight crews and 234 personnel for maintenance and support. The 12th ACS Headquarters and the main operating base were located in III Corps at Bien Hoa. Twelve aircraft located at Bien Hoa covered sorties in support of targets in II Corps, III Corps, and IV Corps. An operating location had been established at Da Nang AB, with an average of six aircraft covering targets in northern II Corps and all of I Corps, from this location. 12/

The relationship of the 12th ACS to the 315th ACW and 834th AD was primarily the result of similarity of aircraft and the related personnel and maintenance requirements. The defoliation mission, however, was totally different from the airlift mission in planning, coordination, and execution. It was essentially the same as a fighter-bomber mission, in that ordnance was delivered on fragged targets under the control of 7AF TACC. Because of the dissimilarity of missions and the fact that the 834th AD was at Tan Son Nhut, the 315th at Phan Rang, and the 12th ACS at Bien Hoa, higher headquarters drew trained personnel from the defoliation mission to be staff advisors. This withdrawal of qualified pilots from the 12th ACS resources would have been unnecessary if the higher headquarters were on the same base. 13/

After consideration of these factors, the Director of Operations, 834th AD concluded in a study dated 12 August 1967 that greater efficiency could be achieved by collocating the 12th ACS with the 315th ACW at Phan Rang. The optimum organization also would have had two operating locations (Bien Hoa

67

and Da Nang) and a reloading point at Phu Cat.[14/]

The Commander, 7AF, approved the selection of Phan Rang AB as the most operationally suitable location for the 12th ACS. Three of the seven additional UC-123 aircraft approved by the Secretary of Defense for deployment to South Vietnam were authorized to beddown at Phan Rang. This brought the strength of the 12th ACS to 25 aircraft, which would be operated from Bien Hoa and Da Nang pending construction of required ramp and support facilities at Phan Rang. An additional eight UC-123 aircraft were requested in support of the FY69/70 MACV herbicide program. A maximum of ten aircraft, of the total 33 requested, was programmed to beddown at Phan Rang. The remainder were to beddown at the Bien Hoa and Da Nang operating locations.[15/]

VNAF Participation

The Director of Operations also discussed in his August study, the possibility of integrating VNAF personnel into the herbicide mission as a means of expanding operations without large adjustments in the USAF manpower ceilings. He explored a concept of training VNAF personnel in the complete mission by integration and on-the-job training for crews and maintenance personnel in the UC-123. However, it appeared that OJT on such a scale in-theater, while conducting a combat operation, and with the inherent language problems and differences in customs, offered a limited chance of success. The concept of having VNAF assume full execution of the crop destruction program offered better possibilities. Under the "Farmgate" policy, VNAF observers were already required to be aboard all crop destruction missions and the aircraft were required to display VNAF markings. The Director of Operations concluded that the VNAF could take over the crop destruction and mosquito spray operations by adapting their C-119 transport squadron on these missions. [16/]

In a letter dated 26 August 1967, 7AF tasked the Air Force Advisory Group to develop a program with a view toward having the "VNAF perform all the crop destruction spray missions, mosquito control missions, and any future program requirements in that order of priority". In a letter to 7AF dated 21 October 1967, the Chief, AFGP, stated that given the proper training and equipment, the VNAF would have the capability to carry out spray operations against mosquito control and crop destruction targets. A firm date could not be determined as to when the VNAF would have been able to assume the mosquito control portion of the mission, but an optimistic estimate was between one and two years after approval of the conversion project was obtained. Over the next several years, he believed the VNAF would be able to assume both the mosquito control and crop destruction mission as proposed by 7AF. [17/]

The Chief, AFGP, however, stated that the impact on the VNAF airlift support capability would have been staggering. Of the three squadrons of C-47 aircraft authorized, one was programmed to convert to AC-47 configuration. Although they would have had a minimal airlift capability, for all practical purposes, airlift support would have been reduced by one-third. This would have been partially offset by the conversion of the 413th TS to C-119 aircraft. To divert 50 percent (eight) of these aircraft, along with the 21 experienced first pilots, to the spray mission would have had a crippling effect on the squadron. There would also have been an impact on the remaining C-47 Transport Squadron, as it was the only available source with the experience level necessary to check out as first pilot in the C-119. Overall, the VNAF pilot strength was 328 below authorized and transport pilot manning was 89 below authorized. In view of this, the Chief, AFGP, recommended that the VNAF not increase participation in the herbicide program beyond its current commitment.[18/]

DMZ Operations

During this period, herbicide operations were extended to the northern portion of the DMZ. Authorization to defoliate specific infiltration routes in this area had been requested by 7AF in August 1966. However, the Secretary of Defense had deferred approval pending an evaluation of world reaction to defoliation operations in the southern part of the DMZ, which had started in February 1967.[19/]

At that time, the Government of Vietnam (at the request of the U.S.) had sent a note to the International Control Commision (ICC), explaining that defoliation had been undertaken as a necessary defensive countermeasure to continuing North Vietnamese violations of the DMZ. However, the situation had changed considerably since that time, and the U.S. did not recommend sending a similar note with respect to defoliation of the northern area of the DMZ. The "demilitarized" Zone was now a hotly contested battle area, and could not under any circumstances be considered "demilitarized". The limited role of the ICC had ceased. Also, most of the present herbicide operations would take place north of the Provisional Military Demarcation Line; i.e., over NVN territory. Consequently, a note to the ICC would have served only the propaganda purpose of Hanoi, which would have charged the U.S. with chemical and biological warfare.[20]

Since no unusual press or political interest had been generated by the missions over the southern half of the DMZ, COMUSMACV was given authority to proceed with defoliation of specific infiltration routes in the northern portion of the DMZ beginning after 25 September. Plans called for defoliation of these routes for a distance of 200 meters on each side of the roads. The operation was to be announced in low key with stress on NVN violation of the DMZ, with the military necessity of defoliation operations as a logical extension of defoliation in the southern part of the DMZ, and the non-deleterious effects of herbicides on human beings or animals.[21]

Effectiveness

Following publication of RAND studies which cast doubt on the effectiveness of chemical crop destruction in Vietnam, JCS and DOD requested the MACV position on pertinent points of the study to evaluate the findings and recommendations.[22]

COMUSMACV reported to CINCPAC that crop destruction operations, which constituted approximately eight percent of the overall herbicide effort, were an integral part of the GVN/US resource denial program in SVN. The GVN at all levels supported the crop destruction operations, which were limited to food-scarce areas in South Vietnam under VC control. The objectives of the program were to:[23]

- Deny food to the VC and VC sympathizers in the immediate area.
- Divert more VC manpower to crop production.

° Place an additional burden on the enemy's logistical system.

° Weaken VC strength, resolve, and morale.

These objectives had met with varying degrees of success. However, intelligence reports indicated that the program had adversely affected the VC/NVA food supply, logistical requirements, and combat effectiveness.

CINCPAC informed the JCS that no program changes were found to be necessary at this time. He stated that the psywar effort in conjunction with the herbicide program had been accelerated in 1967, to gain understanding and support from the civilian population. The areas of South Vietnam were divided into five categories, with the percentage of missions flown in each area indicated below: [24]

```
Uninhabited ........................................ 22%
VC-controlled ...................................... 76%
Contested ..........................................  2%
In the process of being secured ....................  1 sortie
Secured ............................................ None
```

About one-third of the total missions were conducted over or in the immediate vicinity of major VC base areas. All 1967 crop destruction activities were conducted in rice deficient provinces--27 percent in I CTZ; 67 percent in II CTZ; 6 percent in III CTZ; and none in IV CTZ. Approximately 88 percent of all missions were conducted in areas where the population was less than 250 inhabitants per square mile and more than 20 percent in uninhabited areas. [25]

Defections to GVN increased as a result of low morale resulting from food shortages, and also caused some enemy personnel to pretend sickness to avoid fighting. After crop defoliation operations, large numbers of civilians moved to GVN-controlled areas, and as a result, the VC suffered manpower shortages for support purposes.[26/]

An estimated 120,000 short tons of rice and other foods were destroyed through herbicide crop destruction operations during 1967. In several provinces, this constituted at least 80 percent of the crop grown in VC-controlled territory. There were also additional benefits gained from the psychological side effects. The VC apparently believed their own propaganda to the effect that sprayed food and water could not be consumed, and that the spray had a residual effect on the soil. Herbicides were usually 80 percent effective in the destruction of crops, except for certain plants such as potatoes and carrots, which could be salvaged if they were old enough for profitable harvest.[27/]

The loss of foodstuffs and crops often forced the VC/NVA units to look outside of their operational area for their food supply. This placed an additional strain on the enemy's supply system, which often relied heavily on human labor for transportation of goods. The destruction of crops in the fields, the capture of large rice caches, and the combination of defoliation and military operations had kept him on the move, reduced his sources of supply, denied him access to his stores, and disrupted his distribution system. Also, the distribution problem resulting from local shortages was complicated by the loss of cover which restricted freedom of movement during daylight hours.[28/]

Any loss of rice, the most basic and critical food commodity in South Vietnam, inevitably had an important effect upon the enemy's combat effectiveness and the military situation. In some instances, the VC had been forced to divert tactical units to conduct food procurement operations and food transportation tasks. The availability of rice also had to be taken into consideration by the enemy in developing a tactical plan. [29]

CINCPAC concluded that the crop destruction program was an important facet of the resources control program, and its objectives were being met. It was granted that crop destruction did not completely deny food to the VC/NVA, except in certain local situations. However, the major benefit was that the enemy was forced to divert significant amounts of manpower to obtain food. The corps commanders strongly favored continuation of crop destruction operations. A shortcoming in the program was the lack of capability to deliver required sorties in a timely fashion. This shortcoming was being overcome, in part, by the addition of helicopter spray systems and C-123 spray aircraft. While empirical data on the effects of herbicide operations on the VC/NVA were lacking, current intelligence reports established the validity of the program. [30]

CHAPTER VII

PSYCHOLOGICAL WARFARE

The scope and magnitude of the military effort against the enemy in North Vietnam, along the infiltration routes and in South Vietnam, increased requirements for psychological operations support. There were no significant developments in the leaflet dissemination program over South Vietnam. The out-of-country effort included leaflet drops along the Ho Chi Minh Trail in Laos, along the South Vietnam/Cambodia border, and over North Vietnam. The increased demands, particularly for greater coverage of the vital Red River Delta, made it necessary to revaluate the capability of 7AF to meet these requirements with the current delivery system. [1]

Fact Sheet/Frantic Goat

The program of leaflet drops over North Vietnam, formerly known as Fact Sheet, was renamed Frantic Goat in September. The 7AF participation in the program was accomplished by F-4 aircraft from Ubon Royal Thai AB and 315th Air Division C-130 aircraft from Okinawa. Aircraft targeting was provided by MACV, and logistic support of the leaflet program was accomplished by the 7th Psyop Group, Fort Buckner, Okinawa, and the 6th Psyop Battalion, MACV. Program policy and guidance were provided by a committee composed of representatives from the U.S. Embassy, MACV, and the Joint U.S. Public Affairs Office (JUSPAO), with the latter having primary responsibility for development of leaflet themes and texts. [2]

C-130 aircraft were fragged for three Frantic Goat missions per month, with each mission normally requiring three days. The normal C-130A psyload was 24,000 pounds, which equated to 10-16 million leaflets, depending on leaflet size. The majority of the missions were fragged from the DMZ north to Ha Tinh. During the period from July to September, approximately 48 million leaflets per month were dropped in this area. The C-130 aircraft were restricted from operating north of 18° 30' north latitude, from overflight into NVN along the western border, and from flying closer than 20 nautical miles to the NVN east coast. These restrictions generally precluded volume leaflet dissemination north of Vinh, NVN. [3]

The F-4 aircraft were fragged on primary targets in the Red River Delta area and secondary targets in the southern NVN panhandle. These aircraft were restricted from penetrating the high threat areas and were fragged to drop their leaflet bombs at a predetermined point outside the high threat area. This required that the leaflets wind-drift to the desired targets. [4]

The F-4 aircraft normally carried ten M-129-E leaflet bombs. The capacity of the bomb depended on the size of the leaflet, but each bomb could accommodate approximately 80,000 of the standard 3" x 6" leaflet. This equated to approximately 3.2 million leaflets per four-aircraft flight. During the period from July to September 1967, approximately 13.6 million leaflets were dropped by this system. Most of the leaflet dissemination was carried out in the southern panhandle. [5]

Through the combined use of F-4s and C-130s, an average of 61 million leaflets per month were dropped over North Vietnam during the period from July to September 1967, but less than 10 percent of the leaflets were dropped on the Red River Delta. This was due to unfavorable weather; inherent limitations of F-4C aircraft as a leaflet carrier; and an increased number of SAM sites, resulting in a reduction of safe corridors for the F-4. [6/]

Increased Psyops Efforts

The American Embassy noted that the current methods of delivery to the Red River Delta did not disseminate the number of leaflets desired and required for optimum impact on the North Vietnamese population. It appeared that greater efforts had to be made to reach areas of heaviest population; i.e., the Hanoi-Haiphong area. This called for a delivery system which used scheduled and on-call aircraft to meet special situations or specific targets. The Embassy also believed that the delivery system should be less subject to vagaries of weather than the present one. [7/]

JCS and CINCPAC directed that psychological operations in support of the air effort be conducted at a more aggressive pace. On 20 September, CINCPAC issued an operations order for Frantic Goat which stated: [8/]

> *"PACOM and VNAF forces in coordination with American Embassy, Saigon, will conduct overt aerial leaflet operations against selected targets in North Vietnam on a frequent and continuing basis. These operations are designed to reinforce the effects of airstrikes and to accomplish psychological objectives not necessarily related to airstrikes."*

In the event the desired level of leaflet operations could not be achieved by PACAF and VNAF aircraft, it was stipulated that USMC aircraft at Chu Lai, while remaining under operational control of COMUSMACV, would be used. Additionally, CINCPACFLT aircraft were programmed and would be used if necessary, to insure the desired level of operations. [9/]

Authority was granted to conduct Frantic Goat missions in the current ROLLING THUNDER/Iron Hand authorized armed reconnaissance areas. Outside these boundaries the plan called for daytime leaflet drops in the northeastern area to be made in conjunction with ROLLING THUNDER/Iron Hand operations. Occasional night leaflet drops from C-130 aircraft, to be conducted northeast and east of Haiphong using wind drift, were also comtemplated. 10/

COMUSMACV requested 7AF to carry out the following actions:

> *"Increase leaflet drops in the Red River Delta, particularly in the Hanoi-Haiphong target areas, by high performance fighter-bombers and by cargo/bomber-type aircraft rigged for volume saturation loads, using wind drift method. The American Embassy/JUSPAO plans called for delivery of 750 million to 1 billion leaflets into North Vietnam during the period 1 July 1967 to 30 June 1968. Of this total effort, 730 million leaflets at the rate of 60 million per month were to be delivered in the Red River Delta area.*
>
> *"Formalize plans for use of VNAF resources to augment 7AF psyop delivery assets to North Vietnam.*
>
> *"Provide Air Force or Navy leaflet bombs, or alternatives, for VNAF use as required."*

COMUSMACV also stated that there was a requirement for reconnaissance/intelligence activities to determine accuracy of leaflet delivery and impact on target audience, especially in Hanoi and Haiphong. 11/

During the fall of 1967, 7AF made various recommendations to PACAF and COMUSMACV for improving the leaflet delivery capability. In October, a conference was held at Hq 7AF to discuss these proposals and other variables which determined the success or failure of the Frantic Goat program. These included

78

the prevailing winds, leaflet aerodynamic design, and the methods and vehicles which were employed to deliver the leaflets. 12/

Long-range delivery of leaflets was generally difficult to accomplish during the southwest monsoon (Jul-Sep) because of the opposing winds. Overflight, or short range leaflet drift, was the only means of leaflet dissemination. The period of the northeast monsoon (Nov-Apr) was the most opportune time to disseminate psychological leaflets over North Vietnam, especially the Red River Delta. During the transitional periods (May, June, and October), weather conditions were not generally advantageous for psyop activity in the Red River Delta, except for short range wind drift or overflight dissemination. 13/

New Developments

In view of operations restrictions and prevailing winds, 7AF pointed out that a leaflet with very good drift characteristics would be required, particularly for coverage of the Red River Delta. New leaflets could be designed which would be lighter and smaller than those presently in use, which were generally 3" x 6" and printed on relatively heavy paper. A change in leaflet design could result in as much as a 70 percent increase in drift capability and a 600 percent increase in number of leaflets delivered. 14/

B-52s, drones, and balloons had been proposed as alternate means of leaflet delivery. The B-52 could accommodate 42 M-129 leaflet bombs in the high density bomb racks. This payload equated to approximately a four-aircraft flight of F-4s. While the CSAF indicated that the B-52 program was feasible, he stated that other B-52 program parameters must be evaluated prior to implementation. These included:[15/]

- Present CINCPAC/MACV requirement for additional B-52 strike sorties.

- SIOP degradation associated with withdrawal or addition of B-52s from this SIOP posture.

- Overflight restrictions associated with this type aircraft in the proposed area.

- JCS/OSD approval required for additional use of B-52s.

The CSAF reported that missiles such as the MACE and BOMARC-A were evaluated, but were not available in sufficient quantity to support their use as a psyop delivery vehicle. In evaluating the use of drone aircraft, primarily the B-47, it was noted that the necessary modification would cost $500,000 per aircraft and require a one-year lead time. MACV was conducting a study to determine the advisability of using balloons for the dissemination of leaflets in the Red River Delta. This approach, however, posed the problems of limited carrying capacity and unpredictability of delivery.[16/]

On 7 December, MACV requested that 7AF submit a Southeast Asia Operational Requirement (SEAOR) for the following psyops capabilities:

- Development of radio dispensing system.

- Development of increased leaflet dispensing system.

- Development of advanced aerial delivery platforms for dispensing systems.

In addition to delivering increased quantities of leaflets, MACV envisioned the dispensing of small, miniaturized radio receivers in areas of heavy population concentrations, so that individuals could receive live radio broadcasts. A requirement existed for an all-weather airborne vehicle that could effectively operate in a hostile environment and discharge large quantities of psychological material. It was estimated that about a half-million radio receivers would be delivered at varying time intervals in conjunction with leaflet drops, but not necessarily at the same time.[17]

MACV believed that the MK-12, Mod 0 aircraft chemical tank could be used in fighter/bomber-type aircraft as an interim device for dispensing radios. Each tank could hold about 250 radios with chutes, and eight tanks per aircraft would be considered a normal load. Although there were several platforms suitable for the delivery of radio receivers, such as fighter/bomber and C-130-type aircraft, they posed certain limitations. The risks involved in utilizing C-130-type aircraft over hostile territory were unacceptable, even with fighter escort and ECM support. However, this aircraft might possibly be employed in areas adjacent to heavily defended positions provided that wind-drift techniques were used.[18]

The use of the F-4 to deliver 60-million leaflets would require 750 leaflet bombs and 83 aircraft. A year's operation would require 996 aircraft and would cost $1,773,000 in leaflet bombs. Because of the cost and effort required to deliver these leaflets, COMUSMACV felt that a revaluation of current delivery techniques was warranted. He recommended that 7AF take immediate action to provide the following operational requirement:[19]

> *"Develop a compartmentalized leaflet canister or 'tank' to replace the Navy's Model 12 Smoke Tank and to partially or completely replace the M-129E1 leaflet*

> bomb. MACV envisioned that this compartmentalized tank would be used on high performance aircraft for high altitude mass leaflet and radio receiver dissemination using the wind-drift technique. It could also be used for dissemination of gift packages.
>
> "Develop an airlock chamber designed to temporarily replace the troop door on C-130 aircraft for use in high altitude leaflet dissemination missions. The present dissemination system employed a system of rollers, static lines, and break-away boxes and required personnel to use oxygen equipment. The tremendous exertion and use of oxygen required in ejecting the 10-12 tons of leaflets at altitudes of up to 25,000 feet had resulted in cases of hyperventilation, hypoxia, and the bends.
>
> "Consider the introduction of the C-141 aircraft into the aerial dissemination program. Operating with an airlock chamber similar to the one proposed for the C-130, the aircraft could carry 30.5 tons of leaflets on a single pass, providing coverage over tens of thousands of square miles."

MACV suggested that an examination be made of current Air Force assets to determine if a capability were available to satisfy MACV requirements, pending development of a full-scale program and determine if existing assets could be modified on an accelerated basis to meet the operational requirement. At the end of the year, 7AF was preparing a SEAOR for a high volume leaflet and radio dispensing system.[20]

Cambodian Border Test

Psychological operations against NVA/VC forces in the Cambodian border area were being conducted on a trial basis during this period. Plans for these operations had been proposed in the fall of 1966 and approved by JCS in March 1967, for a six-month period.[21]

The following guidelines applied to these operations:[22]

"Leaflet drops might be accomplished by overflying the target area, or by using wind drift technique.

"Overflights were authorized in that area of Cambodia along the South Vietnam border from 12-30N, north to Laos, and extending 20-km into Cambodia. Leaflet delivery flights into the area would be accomplished by cargo-type aircraft, at night, and between 6-10,000 feet AGL. A minimum of four overflight sorties per week was authorized.

"The wind drift technique was used to disseminate leaflets into that area of Cambodia along the South Vietnam border from 12-00N 106-25E, north to Laos, and extending 20-km into Cambodia."

The six-month test period was concluded on 13 September 1967. A review and evaluation of the program, submitted to CINCPAC on 5 October, recommended a continuation of the program for an indefinite period. A total of 75,251,000 leaflets had been disseminated, during the test period. An analysis conducted to determine the effectiveness of the test showed inconclusive results. However, there was some limited evidence, provided by ralliers, that the leaflets were being read and had some influence on members of the target audience. Continuation of the program for an indefinite period was authorized by CINCPAC on 3 November 1967.[23]

CHAPTER VIII

BASE DEFENSE

Enemy attacks against air bases continued to present formidable problems during the second half of 1967. Because of the vast areas within range of modern weapons in the rocket/mortar category, air bases were particularly vulnerable to this type of attack. During July-December 1967, the enemy launched seven attacks against four of the ten USAF bases in-country, which made a total of 15 attacks for the year. Loss and damage to fixed and rotary-wing aircraft for all services during 1967 were 76 destroyed and 414 damaged. [1]

Da Nang

Da Nang AB, which had been hit on 27 February and 15 March, was attacked again on 15 July. Prior to the attack, numerous intelligence reports had been received of enemy plans to hit the base. USMC units engaged in a firefight with elements of a sapper unit on 30 June 1967, and a subsequent sweep of the area, revealed the enemy was attempting either to store rockets in the area for later use, or they were attempting to set up and fire rockets into Da Nang AB. At the time of the sweep, four enemy bodies were found along with two 140-mm rockets. [2]

The enemy, reportedly an unidentified NVA unit, launched an 122-mm rocket attack against the base at approximately 0020H on 15 July. It was impossible to determine the exact duration of the attack, due to secondary explosions in the south and southwest areas of the base, but it probably lasted about 20 minutes. During this time, an estimated 83 rounds hit the

84

airfield proper. Counterfire commenced approximately one minute after the first rounds were launched. AC-47 aircraft provided suppressive fire and illumination until daylight. 3/

Enemy firing positions were in groups of six and located in tree lines, in close proximity to hamlets or friendly units. The choice of positions was probably intended to prevent mass retaliatory fire. Positions for the rocket launcher required minimum preparation and they could be fired from almost any terrain. Rounds were delivered in ripples of six, fired at staggered intervals, apparently as a defense against immediate counterfire. There was some evidence that the rockets might have been carried into the firing positions some time prior to the attack and buried in position. 4/

As a result of the attack, eight USAF personnel were killed; 88 U.S. personnel and 1 VNAF individual were hospitalized; and 51 USAF personnel were treated and released. A total of eight USAF aircraft were destroyed and 35 were damaged. The VNAF wing did not sustain any aircraft damage, but the USMC had two aircraft destroyed and two damaged. Property damage was assessed at approximately $1.5 million, which included damaged or destroyed dormitories, dining hall, water plant, laundry, power plant, air freight and passenger terminals, hangar, warehouses, storage areas, etc. 5/

In view of this attack against Da Nang AB and the expected increase of enemy activity during the RVN election period, a reappraisal of I Corps airfield passive defense measures was undertaken. The following specific actions were recommended for immediate implementation: 6/

- Reduce airfield aircraft density to the maximum extent possible.

- Bunker and disperse aircraft to the maximum extent possible.

- Reduce transient elements to a minimum and decrease as much as practicable the numbers of personnel in the immediate airfield areas.

- Maintain maximum internal/interior security against enemy intelligence efforts to fix target locations.

- Conduct maximum training and exercise of interior and perimeter security personnel.

- Review the systems and procedures in effect for the storage, assembly, and loading of aircraft ordnance to minimize danger from secondary explosions; arm only the aircraft required to meet alert and mission requirements.

- Insure readiness to execute fire and disaster control procedures.

- Indoctrination and training of personnel to minimize casualties and damage to aircraft and equipment.

The next attack against Da Nang Air Base occurred on 2 September. Numerous intelligence reports had indicated that the base would be attacked prior to the 3 September 1967 presidential election. At 0050H on 2 September, the base was subjected to a 140-mm rocket attack which lasted less than 30 seconds. An estimated nine rockets struck within the Air Force side of Da Nang AB, the majority of the rounds landing in one general area. Three USAF personnel were hospitalized and five were treated and released. Six USAF aircraft were damaged, none was destroyed. USMC and VNAF wings did not sustain aircraft damage. Three structures received minor damage.[7/]

When Da Nang was attacked for the fifth time on 9 September, it achieved the dubious distinction of having sustained more hits during 1967 than any other USAF base. Prior to the attack, various intelligence reports had indicated the presence of a Sapper Battalion in the vicinity of the base, which was equipped with rockets and presumably had the mission of attacking the Da Nang installation. At approximately 0005 hours on 9 September, the base came under a 30-second rocket attack. Three 140-mm rockets struck within the Air Force side of the base. As a result, two USAF personnel were killed; three were hospitalized; and seven were treated and released. Two USAF and one VNAF aircraft were damaged. Four structures received minor damage. A sweep of the launch area revealed that the enemy left eleven launchers and eight unfired 140-mm rockets in firing position.[8/]

Nha Trang

An increase in terrorist activities and sightings of suspected VC movement had been noted prior to the 10 October 1967 attack against Nha Trang AB and the 5th Special Forces Group Headquarters. However, there were no significant reports of enemy sightings or movement on the night of 9 October 1967, that would have indicated an attack was imminent. The attack apparently was launched from a position approximately 2,500 meters west of Nha Trang AB in a low, swampy area. No positive contact was made and enemy withdrawal routes could not be determined. The enemy used two 82-mm mortars in the attack, both targeted on the west perimeter of the base and the 5th Special Forces compound. The installation received 16 rounds of 82-mm mortar fire, four of which failed to explode. Damage to Air Force property amounted to three small craters in the northeast-southwest runway and slight shrapnel damage to one wooden frame building. The Special Forces compound received seven rounds of 82-mm mortar fire, resulting in one Huey helicopter damaged beyond repair and three other helicopters receiving minor shrapnel damage.[9]

Following the pattern previously established, VC terrorist activities in the Nha Trang area increased in number and intensity before the 26 November attack. In addition, there were reports indicating that additional personnel were supplementing the strength of the K-90 Sapper Unit targeted against Nha Trang. During the five-minute attack which began at 0010H on 26 November, the air base received a total of 29 82-mm mortar and one 75-mm recoilless rifle rounds; one 82-mm mortar and one 75-mm recoilless rifle round failed to explode. Casualties consisted of five USAF and 16 U.S. Army WIA. There was no damage to the runway and taxiways and only minor damage to aircraft parking areas. One C-130 aircraft was destroyed, another heavily damaged, and two lightly damaged. Two AC-47s, two O-2Bs, and two Army HU-1D helicopters also received minor damage, and two buildings in the Special Forces compound were lightly damaged.[10]

Bien Hoa

A 60-mm mortar attack against Bien Hoa AB and Binh Hoa village, adjacent to the west perimeter of the air base, was carried out from 2240-2244 hours on 5 November. The follow-up counteraction continued until 0045 hours on 6 November. A small, hostile force, estimated to be two platoons in strength, expended approximately fifteen 60-mm mortar rounds against the base. U.S. casualties consisted of one U.S. Army and one USAF wounded. Regional and Popular Forces suffered one KIA and five wounded. One ARVN dependent was wounded off-base. There was no damage to aircraft and only minor damage to equipment and facilities.[11]

Tuy Hoa

After several months of relative inactivity in the immediate vicinity of Tuy Hoa AB, the enemy gradually increased offensive and terroristic activity in August. These activities were presumably designed to disrupt the 3 September presidential election. However, there were also intelligence reports pointing to a "Tuy Hoa Resurrection Campaign". This campaign was to be a concerted effort by NVA and VC to restore the Communist position and influence in the Tuy Hoa Valley. There were no reports of enemy sightings or significant enemy movement on the night of 6 September that would have signaled the attack. The enemy used two 57-mm recoilless rifles, a B-40 rocket, two light machine guns, and a number and variety of small-arms. They positioned the weapons in a small grove of trees and directed the 57-mm recoilless rifles toward District Headquarters and the two machine guns toward the air base in the opposite direction. 12/

The attack began at 0047H on 7 September, when two observation towers and one gun bunker on the northwest perimeter of the base reported receiving heavy automatic weapons fire from four to five enemy positions. At 0050H, District Headquarters reported that the VC were attacking in a "human wave", and this attack lasted about 60 minutes. Air support in the form of gunships and flareships (which arrived on the scene within 20 minutes) fired into the enemy positions. Sentries at several other posts reported small groups of enemy personnel. At approximately 0200H, the enemy terminated his attack and attempted to withdraw from the area. Contact with the enemy was broken off at 0345H. Friendly casualties consisted of one Security Policeman killed and three MACV advisors wounded. The enemy suffered eight KIA (three by body count). There was no damage to aircraft or facilities.[13]

One AC-47 gunship, Spooky 32, orbited the area during the time of the attack. The flight commander was in an observation tower overlooking the activity and directed flare drops and gunship strikes on the enemy position. Two Huey gunships from Phu Hiep Army Airfield were called by MACV; they each expended ordnance into the enemy position. At 0315H, Spooky departed and Moonshiner 35, a flareship, was used to provide illumination through the rest of the night.[14]

Base Defense Seminar

The numerous attacks against air bases during 1967, made increased protection of air resources in Vietnam a pressing requirement which received high level attention. On 17 July 1967, the Deputy COMUSMACV directed the establishment of project managers at MACV and the four CTZs to coordinate the effort and to take an in-depth look at the problem of rocket attacks. Immediate actions included conduct of a command-wide Project Managers' meeting held on 25 July, and the establishment of a MACV investigation team to conduct on-the-spot examinations following any future rocket attacks. Steps were also taken to review and refine plans pertaining to rocket defense; to review the Revolutionary Development Program in areas adjacent to installations; to increase psychological operations; and to assist appropriate agencies in procurement of equipment and resources that might be applicable to the overall problem of rocket defense.[15]

Numerous interacting military, geographic, and socio-political factors, unique to the Vietnam environment, complicated the task of base defense. The size and nature of the 500 square kilometers of terrain lying within rocket range (10 kilometers) of each base in Vietnam prohibited continuous monitoring to prevent launch of a standoff attack. The air bases at Nha Trang, Pleiku, Da Nang, and Saigon were located within or adjacent to large urban concentrations. In many instances, the base perimeter fence abutted private dwellings or public roads. Other bases had densely populated areas within ten kilometers. Adjacent urban areas afforded the enemy reconnaissance, and intelligence collection points made it difficult to keep the area under surveillance, and provided cover for enemy attacks. 16/

More than half of the major USAF air bases in Vietnam were owned and controlled by the Vietnamese Air Force (VNAF), despite the preponderance of American forces, equipment, and facilities on them. The VNAF Base Commander had legal responsibility for overall base defense. He controlled access to and egress from the base by foot, vehicle, and aircraft. Naturally, the Vietnamese Commander operated the base by the regulations, customs, and ethics of his own culture, which did not always coincide with the American way of doing things. 17/

Command and control also presented other problems which detracted from a maximum defense posture. Friendly military forces had been limited in their ability to apply immediate, large-scale punitive action against the enemy force which could have served as a deterrent to future attacks. Whenever a threat developed to any installations, permission had to be granted, in most cases by the Province Chief, to engage the enemy target. 7AF believed this concept was militarily unacceptable; it resulted in unnecessary delays in bringing punitive action to bear. In a presentation at the Command-wide Base Defense Seminar on 12 June 1967, 7AF emphasized the importance of having a fully coordinated plan in effect, which permitted the commitment of all available resources, under a central command function, to repel and punish any enemy force. The senior tactical commander in the area must have the command authority to commit all necessary forces without recourse to other authority. [18/]

In Vietnam, the Army was responsible for the external protection of all Air Force bases, except Da Nang, which was a Marine Corps responsibility. Army and Marine air bases were generally located within a large Army or Marine Tactical Area of Responsibility (TAOR), providing the commander with space to defend his base in depth. However, the Army frequently did not occupy the TAOR adjacent to the Air Force base. Also, since the Army had a higher priority mission of active pursuit of the enemy, it did not deploy a significant number of troops in a static defense role around USAF bases. The Air Force defended only the interior of the base up to the perimeter and did not defend the exterior out to the 10-km rocket range. The USAF air base commander had no command authority or operational control over the forces, if any, within 10-km of his base (an area of 500 square kilometers from which mortar and rocket attacks could be launched, unless he had been able to work out a special defense zone or a joint defense plan with the adjacent force commander. [19/]

Seventh Air Force believed it might be advisable to reexamine the traditional concept of limiting Air Force responsibility to internal security of its installations, with external defense being assigned to other friendly military forces. The proposal was made that the USAF total area of security responsibility be extended to encompass an area 4,000 meters from the center of major 7AF installations. If this concept were employed, it would free friendly ground forces from the immediate perimeters of the installations and permit them to provide better coverage of the areas from which the threat of long-range rockets occurred. To accomplish this change in responsibility, 7AF pointed out it would be necessary to completely sanitize the area out to the 4,000 meter ring; i.e., remove all indigenous personnel, shops, villages, etc., and defoliate completely. The additional territory would be controlled through the use of advanced detection equipment and small unit air and ground assault forces. This would require tactical security support equipment such as multi-purpose concealed intrusion devices, air base surveillance radar, battlefield illumination systems, and other devices. In addition, crew-served weapons, armored personnel carriers, and related equipment would be needed. There would also be a requirement for sufficient fixed-wing aircraft and helicopters assigned solely to the security role to permit instantaneous response to alarmed areas. In addition, 7AF recommended that security police manpower authorizations be increased in a limited amount to provide sufficient response forces for this area and that USAF and VNAF security forces be completely integrated.[20]

7AF also considered the use of additional airpower in the base defense role. The AC-47 Dragonship, utilizing firepower in conjunction with an illumination capability, had been successfully employed in defense of fixed installations and in support of nearby friendly operations. Several aircraft, including the C-54, C-118, C-7, and C-130, were considered for follow-on to the

AC-47, or to provide an interim additional capability. All the aircraft were considered unsuitable, with the exception of the C-130 and C-118, the latter to be used as an interim aircraft pending C-130 availability. The C-130 would provide sufficient speed and maneuverability to accommodate the additional ammunition/flare load and a standoff capability of approximately 10,000 feet altitude.[21/]

Any aircraft utilized in direct support of installation security should have the capability to observe, detect, discriminate, and destroy, and to a limited extent the AC-47 provided these capabilities. However, more effective firepower and mobility capability could be developed through the use of armed helicopters in conjunction with the AC-47. 7AF recommended that helicopters be provided solely in a base defense role and that they be placed under the command of the tactical commander responsible for the defense of the installation.[22/]

In considering other uses of airpower in the base defense role, 7AF suggested that consideration be given to utilizing operational aircraft such as the F-100 and A-1E for partial duty in a security role. Although this would lessen tactical strike capability, it would greatly increase the punitive capability in support of fixed installations. It also recommended more extensive use of forward air controllers in the 11,000 meter range of major installations; increased day and night photographic reconnaissance; more intensive use of light intensification devices to enhance detection capability; and an increase in the defense posture of major installations.[23/]

The CG, USARV, issued guidelines for both active and passive defense measures to all four CTZs. The guidance placed high priority on the revetment buildup program, aircraft dispersion, perimeter defense installations, and the maximum use of ground towers. Active defense measures focused upon counter-mortar radar and airborne defenses. Airborne forces had proved an effective means of locating enemy firing positions. At critical airfields, designated aircraft were to be placed on three-minute ground alert during hours of darkness. In addition, patrol operations, searches, and ambushes would be extended out to the limit of effective enemy weapon range.[24/]

CHAPTER IX

NORTH VIETNAM AIR DEFENSE SYSTEM

North Vietnam continued to systematically expand and intensify its air defense structure, which included AAA/AW, SAMs, MIGs, and an efficient radar and command and control system. This formidable air defense system resulted in 109 USAF aircraft lost to enemy action during the period 1 July-31 December 1967 (July - 18; August - 23; October - 21; November - 26; and December - 10). The overall USAF loss rate in North Vietnam in 1967, however, was lower than in 1966, as indicated below: 1/

	1966	1967
Sorties	68,481	86,071
Losses	172	191
Rate per 1,000 sorties	2.5	2.2

Antiaircraft Artillery

Of the 119 USAF aircraft lost in Route Packages V and VI during the year, 25 were attributed to SAMs, 21 to MIG aircraft, and the remainder presumed lost to enemy ground fire. Practically all losses in other Route Packages were also due to enemy ground fire. AAA thus continued to be the most effective element of the North Vietnam Air Defense capability, with RP I and RP VI being the most heavily defended areas. The mobility of AAA weapons made it almost impossible to predict with any degree of certainty which of the sites would be active at any given time. The weapons themselves could be emplaced in a matter of minutes and shifted quite rapidly within the RP VI area to mass fire around those targets which the North Vietnamese felt needed greatest protection. RP VIA, in particular, with its large number of weapons, small geographic area, and close target groupings, was a giant flak trap.[2/]

The 37-mm gun was the smallest caliber weapon in the NVN inventory that was still classed as antiaircraft artillery. It was often found in groups of four guns per battery, but it was also quite common to find five or seven guns. The 37-mm guns were frequently deployed in revetments that were originally prepared for 57-mm guns. The ground near the site might appear relatively undisturbed due to the absence of radar and reduced support requirements. Gun crews took various measures to protect themselves, including construction of a "Beehive" site in which the sides of the revetments were extended and actually formed an igloo shape with the roof left open.[3/]

The 57-mm gun was most numerous in the NVN AAA inventory and had nearly four times the range of the 37-mm (19,700 feet against 5,600 feet). The 57-mm gun could be used as a radar fire-controlled weapon or fired manually. The normal 57-mm site had six revetments for weapons, and at least two revetments for the fire-control radar and director. Revetted generators and ammunition storage areas might also be present at the sites along with trenches used for crew protection and AW positions.[4/] Figure 8 reveals an eight-position battery with five positions occupied. Related electronic and radar equipment is also located in the area.

The 85-mm AAA guns were the hardest to identify, due to the similarity between the 57-mm and 85-mm weapons. Although photography revealed relatively slight physical differences between the 85-mm and 57-mm guns, the effectiveness of the two weapons was quite different. The 85-mm gun had an effective anti-aircraft range of 27,500 feet. It pushed a 21-pound projectile to its maximum self-destruction range of 34,540 feet, while the 57-mm pushed a six-pound projectile to its maximum self-destruction range of 23,736 feet. It was formerly believed that these guns were always utilized with radar fire-control, but pilots returning from raids over the Mu Gia Pass reported 85-mm bursts from sites which did not contain fire-control radar. Without a requirement for radar, the 85-mm guns would be easier to take cross-country, to emplace, and to maintain. This would reduce the complexity of the sites and make them harder to detect. [5/]

The total occupied gun positions in NVN in July were as follows: [6/]

	ROUTE PACKAGES						
	I	II	III	IV	V	VI	VII
TOTAL POSITIONS	6,858	3,439	3,485	3,509	3,620	10,315	34,632
TOTAL POSITIONS OCCUPIED	1,274	470	605	752	1,029	4,381	8,511

Enemy efforts to intensify infiltration of troops and equipment through the DMZ resulted in a steadily increasing number of U.S. armed reconnaissance sorties in that area and RP I. To support its infiltration effort and to counter air attacks, the enemy increased the number of guns in RP I by 175 during July. This represented almost the total increase for the entire country. The total number of positions rose from 6,540 in June to 6,858 in July, and the number of occupied positions increased from 1,099 to 1,274. [7/]

Enemy searchlight activity appeared to be receiving increased emphasis

EIGHT POSITION AAA BATTERY
FIGURE 8

at this time, but proved fairly ineffective against U.S. strike missions. There were 41 reports of searchlights in NVN in the period from 1 April 1967, to the middle of August. The largest concentration of lights was along the northwest railroad between Phu Tho and Yen Bai. Of the 18 reported instances of searchlight activity in this area, eight were associated with intense AA fire, and most were thought to be tracking the aircraft. In addition, Tachi I Beam/Track searchlight radars were noted active on two occasions. Early in the morning of 20 July, an Iron Hand/Commando Nail flight encountered 25 searchlights and extremely heavy flak in the Yen Bai area. According to pilots' reports, these searchlights lit up the entire valley and provided a degree of illumination comparable to that seen over major air terminal cities. In addition to the Yen Bai area, searchlights were reported as far south as Vinh, and as far northeast as Kep. [8]

The enemy AAA buildup in the southern portion of the country continued in August. The number of gun positions in RP I increased by 336 guns, more than tripling the January figure of 521. There were slight decreases in gun positions in RP V and VIA; some of these guns probably were relocated to the southern Route Package areas to provide increased firepower. However, the aircraft loss rate in RP I, which had increased from 0.4 per 1,000 attack sorties in January to 2.2 in July, dropped to 1.5 in August. [9]

Although the total number of AAA guns and positions increased only slightly during September, emphasis continued on RP I. During the month, the enemy gained 168 guns, 119 of which were in RP I. In October, the AAA structure decreased, primarily in the northernmost Route Packages. This decrease could be attributed either to bombing effects, dismantling by the enemy, or possibly to better photographic coverage, subsequent improved photo readout, and more accurate "gun counts". [10/]

In November, there was a small decrease in occupied gun positions, but a significant increase in total gun positions. The reduction in guns was fairly evenly distributed throughout all Route Packages; however, the increase in positions was predominantly in RP VIA and B. The Air Force loss rate in RP I during November was 2.2. This was approximately three times the October rate and was equal to the July high. To date, 45 attack aircraft had been lost in RP I for a loss rate of 1.3. [11/]

There were no drastic changes in the AAA/AW structure in December. The total number of guns decreased by 136, while the number of gun positions increased by 595. The greatest change occurred in Route Package I where a decrease of 155 guns was noted. The AAA structure in NVN at the end of the year was as follows: [12/]

ROUTE PACKAGE AREA

	I	II	III	IV	V	VIA	VIB	TOTAL
January 1967								
TOTAL POSITIONS	4,781	3,381	2,749	2,681	2,999	7,709	4,526	28,826
TOTAL OCCUPIED POSITIONS	521	391	511	730	834	2,526	1,613	7,126
December 1967								
TOTAL POSITIONS	7,440	3,378	3,498	3,585	3,493	10,827	4,182	36,303
TOTAL OCCUPIED POSITIONS	1,512	603	625	594	1,030	2,578	888	7,830

During 1967, the total number of guns increased by more than 700 and the prepared gun positions increased by about 7,500. In RP I, the enemy tripled the number of guns and made a substantial increase in the number of gun positions. Also, 85-mm guns were used in the vicinity of the DMZ for the first time, posing a threat to high flying aircraft. The guns in RP VIA increased slightly, while a considerable decrease occurred in RP VIB. Possibly more reliance may have been placed on the MIG/SAM defense in this area, thereby permitting the transfer of AAA to RP I. [13]

Camouflage

In the face of increasing air attacks, the North Vietnamese displayed a high degree of sophistication in the use of new camouflage techniques. They had a thorough knowledge of deception practices and demonstrated ingenuity at blending equipment into the natural surroundings. The enemy's deception campaign was intended to counter the intensive U.S. reconnaissance efforts, and the North Vietnamese were apparently well aware of the limitations of photo interpretation and of reconnaissance system capabilities. [14]

In one case, three AAA sites, probably light caliber guns, were grouped within a 200-meter radius along the northwest rail line in RP V. The concentration of 20 guns in such a small area was normally an invitation for an airstrike. However, in this case, the weapons were so well camouflaged that the area was not reported on the initial readout of the film. The pilot was probably unaware of the sites until they fired upon him. In another example of successful deception, the North Vietnamese made a Hound helicopter appear to be a part of a field pattern. From the oblique, the body of the helicopter was clearly visible. The drapings on the rotors appeared to be ineffectual. But, viewed from above, rotors became dividing lines in a small farm patch between two groups of huts. The body was merely a broader line among many dividing lines, and the camouflage was very effective. 15/

SAMs

During 1967, the number of prepared SAM sites in NVN increased from 151 to 270; a gain of 119 sites. Since 41 of these sites were not in use, the number of known sites at the end of the year was 229. North Vietnam was estimated to have 25 SA-2 battalions, but only 23 of them were believed to be in firing position at any one time and were an active threat to U.S. aircraft. 16/

The 3,484 SAMs expended in 1967 were more than triple those expended in 1966; there were 17 times as many as were fired in 1965. However, effectiveness declined as the average number of SAMs expended to down one U.S. aircraft increased as shown below:

	1965	1966	1967	TOTAL
Missiles Fired	200	1,096	3,484	4,780
Losses	11	34	64	109
Kill Ratio	18.2	32.2	54.4	43.9

Significant developments in SAM employment was their concentration around Hanoi and increased use of hastily prepared field positions near the DMZ. These factors made the SAM battalions more difficult to locate, but they were also less effective. 17/

There were three known SAM support facilities in North Vietnam. They were located at Haiphong, Hai Duong, and Ha Gia, with a possible additional facility at Can Nau. In addition, there were seven suspected sites. A SAM support facility was responsible for missile assembly, storage, checkout, and movement of the Guideline SA-2 missiles to and from launch sites. The support facility was normally manned by an 186-man support battalion and could prepare about 20 missiles in 24 hours. It could fully check out ten missiles in the same period. Sustained operation of the SA-2 system was, therefore, dependent upon the support battalion's ability to prepare and transport ready missiles to the firing battalions. [18]

On the basis of photographic evidence alone, it appeared that there were no facilities capable of performing a missile support function at five of the seven suspected sites (An Cho, 2120N 10651E; Ben Quang, 170323N 1065326E; Kep, 211927N 1061518E; Thanh Hoa, 201025N 1055309E; and Xom Le, 210058N 1055452E). At Phuc Yen Southwest (211234N 1054753E), the presence of SA-2 missile canisters, nose cones and shipping crates, missile transporters, and a mobile crane suggested that the area might be serving as a missile support facility. Many of the typical elements of the normal facility were lacking, however, such as drive-through buildings, wide-radius turns in the road system, and a revetted area for warhead and fuzing storage. Also lacking were fuel and oxidizer storage areas. The presence of a large number of missile canisters and shipping crates at the Vinh Yen facility (2119N 10538E) suggested a more complicated role than mere storage. Additional information was needed, however, to determine positively if they were serving as SAM support facilities. [19]

Hanoi apparently still believed that the dangers involved in SAM operations in and near the DMZ were worth the high risk. Indications of an enemy SAM capability were first noted in February 1967, when SAM transporter equipment was observed moving southward, and Fan Song signals were detected later in the month. Seventh Air Force reported in its Weekly Air Intelligence Summary:[20]

> "The SA-2 battalions operating in the vicinity of the DMZ are probably quite autonomous. Since the NVN MIG force does not operate that far south, it is not necessary for the battalion to coordinate its attacks with higher authority. When a lucrative target appears, the battalion can simply shoot and scoot. Within about three hours after launching an attack, the battalion can be in order and proceeding to a new site."

The 256 SAM firings reported during July were an increase of 51 over June, but they did not approach the record high of 409 reached in May. Most of the firings were directed at Navy and Marine aircraft and resulted in the loss of six of their aircraft and damage to five. Of the relatively few missiles fired at Air Force aircraft, most were fired at reconnaissance aircraft and their escorts. No missiles had been fired at daylight strike forces penetrating into RP VI directly from Thailand since 11 June. This pattern seemed to indicate that the ECM protective envelope generated by the strike aircraft was more effective in discouraging SAM activity than were the countermeasures of the reconnaissance aircraft and their small overall force. Also, the disproportionately large number of missiles fired at Navy ALQ-51-equipped aircraft seemed to indicate that they provided the enemy a better target than QRC-160/ALQ-71-equipped aircraft.[21]

The 402 SA-2 missile firings in August resulted in the loss of two USAF and six Navy aircraft. An RF-4C downed on 12 August was the first pod-equipped Air Force aircraft lost to a SAM since 27 May. As in July, a greater number of missiles were directed against Navy aircraft.[22]

SAM firings dropped to 169 in September, and, of these, 73 were directed at Air Force aircraft. This was the lowest number of firings reported since the March figure of 138. One Air Force RF-4C and one Navy A-4 aircraft were lost. The kill ratio per missile fired for September was 84.5:1. This compared very favorably with a ratio of 18.2:1 for 1965 and 32.2:1 for 1966. [23]

The first firing of SAMs against B-52s occurred on 17 September. Two EB-66s in the area intercepted Fan Song tracking and guidance signals and issued SAM warnings. The flight of B-52s was just south of the DMZ at 37,000-38,000 feet, inbound to a target north of the DMZ. The B-52s also intercepted the tracking and guidance signals, employed jamming, and took evasive action. Shortly thereafter, two SAMs were observed emerging from the undercast and detonated at .5NM and 1.5NM from the formation. No damage was sustained and the aircraft proceeded to an alternate target. [24]

The 522 SAMs reported in October established a new record and were almost one-half the number fired for the entire year of 1966. The large number of missiles (340) directed at Air Force aircraft represented a reversal of the previous trend when the majority of the SAM firings were directed at Navy aircraft. On 29 October, a B-52 flight reported SAM firings near the DMZ; the flight took evasive action, and no damage was sustained by the B-52s or the F-105 escort. The largest number of missiles fired at a reconnaissance flight during 1967 occurred on 22 October, when 16 SAMs were directed at a single RF-4C reconnaissance flight and its F-4D escorts. [25]

Although the number of SAMs fired during November decreased to 343, they established a new loss record of nine Air Force and three Navy aircraft. Also, the 94 SAM firings reported on 19 November set a record high for a single day's activity. The number of firings continued to decrease in December, as did their effectiveness. Of the 247 SAM firings reported during that month, 180 were directed at Air Force aircraft. In the middle of December, the Air Force had initiated several operational and electronic techniques to reduce SAM effectiveness which were apparently proving successful. Among the measures initiated was an increase in the number of jamming pods, including a special pod designed to jam the SAM beacon (missile tracking frequency), lowered ECM pod settings to 2,880 MHz, and increased active ECM support. Also, the number of IRON HAND missions was increased, and a multiple axis of approach to targets was utilized. [26]

On 20 December nine B-52 aircraft on an ARC LIGHT mission near the DMZ reported two probable SAMs and their detonations at 32,000-36,000 feet. The other two occasions of SAMs fired at B-52s occurred on 17 September and 29 October. Up to the end of 1967, two Marine A-4s and an Air Force O-1 had been downed by SAMs in the DMZ area, but no B-52s had been lost or damaged by SAMs. [27]

MIGs

The high level of MIG activity in May and early June was followed by decreased activity in July. The 12 MIG engagements, eight sightings, and one encounter during that month represented 50 percent of the June level. There were no specific reasons for the disengagement, except that the enemy usually followed a period of heavy aircraft losses with decreased MIG aggressiveness. [28]

By August, the picture had changed again. MIG attacks against

Navy aircraft on 10 and 13 August resulted in two enemy aircraft destroyed. The remaining MIG attacks during August were directed against Air Force aircraft. The enemy clearly demonstrated a well-coordinated ground-controlled intercept capability. On 23 August MIG-21s shot down two F-4Ds during a strike against the Yen Vien rail yard. The MIGs came out of a cloud layer at 25,000 feet, made a single pass from the rear, and fired three air-to-air missiles, downing the F-4Ds. The MIGs then climbed back into the overcast and disappeared. In all, there were 16 MIG engagements, 20 encounters, and 15 sightings during the month. The score for the air-to-air war since the beginning of the year was 62 enemy losses to 13 friendly losses, a ratio of 4.8:1. [29]

The first U.S. engagement with Chinese Communist MIGs over NVN also took place during August. On the 13th at 1245H, a Navy F-4B was participating in a search and rescue effort in the vicinity of 2149N 10744E, when the pilot was attacked by four MIG-19s. Two of the MIGs fired a total of four missiles at the F-4, and another MIG-19 made a cannon-firing pass before the Navy aircraft broke down into the clouds and egressed the area. The MIG-19s were probably from Ningming Airfield in south China, located only 12NM from the North Vietnam border. [30]

From August until the end of the year, the North Vietnamese Air Force showed increasing willingness to range farther from the Hanoi area in their efforts to shoot down U.S. aircraft. The proportion of the encounters in RPs IV and V increased gradually during August, September, and October, and jumped sharply in November. Although some of this increase might be attributable to increased strike activity in RP V because of marginal weatner in RP VIA, it emphasized MIG aggressiveness in the employment of guerrilla tactics and the improved GCI capability of NVN. 31/

The MIGs attacked only when the tactical situation appeared to be positively in their favor. They used surprise, made maximum use of concealment, and generally employed hit and run tactics, unless they had decisive numerical and tactical superiority. The attacking MIGs generally outnumbered U.S. aircraft by two to one. MIGs concentrated on small reconnaissance, strike, or Iron Hand flights. By capitalizing on his GCI advantage, the enemy MIG force was able to attack without being seen, as in the case of the F-4Ds shot down on 23 August. The MIG tactics were effective to a degree. In September, 48 aircraft were forced to jettison ordnance as a defensive measure when attacked. This was the highest number in 1967, almost double the previous high of 28 in one month. During the month, there were 16 air-to-air engagements, 5 encounters, and 29 sightings, for a total of 50 incidents. 32/

Normally, MIG-17s were not vectored away from the airfield/target area for the purpose of attacking strike aircraft; this tactic was left to the MIG-21s. The MIG-17s usually operated in two flights of four aircraft each. One flight would orbit in the vicinity of the target at low altitude, 1,500 to 3,500 feet, and would attempt to engage strike aircraft during the target run and on the subsequent pulloff. The second flight of four MIG-17s would orbit at higher altitudes (9,000 to 15,000 feet) in the same general area as the first flight of MIG-17s, and would strike aircraft at the start of their bomb run, using cloud cover or the sun to best advantage. These flights of

MIG-17s were almost always centered between the target which U.S. strike aircraft were bombing and the sensitive area which they were defending; they were aggressive when strike aircraft flew into their immediate area.[33/]

The attack against the Phuc Yen Airfield on 24 October resulted in five MIG-21s and seven MIG-15/17s destroyed or damaged on the ground and extensive damage to the runways and support facilities. At the beginning of 1967, North Vietnam had approximately 70 MIGs. By the end of October, strikes had been authorized and conducted against all MIG airfields except Gia Lam. From this time until the end of the year, only about 20 aircraft were operating from airfields in North Vietnam, with the balance operating from Chinese bases.[34/]

During November, MIG activity remained at approximately the October level with 23 engagements, 24 encounters, and 23 sightings. MIGs downed three F-105s, one F-4D, and two F-4Bs, with a loss of two MIG-17s and a damaged MIG-21. In the period 16-30 November, the Air Force lost 15 aircraft (nine F-105s, four RF-4Cs, and two F-4Cs). The Air Force experienced 198 SAM firings during that period with a new record number of firings for a single day being established on 19 November. On that date, the Air Force reported 94 firings during strikes on six targets in the Hanoi area, resulting in four downed aircraft. Because of these heavy losses, a conference was held at PACAF to evaluate enemy tactics and capabilities. The findings indicated that the losses could be due to a combination of factors. They stated that the "increased density of Hanoi SAM defenses, coupled with well-coordinated MIG attacks to disrupt Iron Hand, increased SAM effectiveness. It is virtually impossible to penetrate without jamming 'burn thru' being available to some

109

sites". The conferees recommended that:[35]

- Iron Hand and MIG CAP forces be doubled for strikes in the high threat area.
- Strike forces enter the Hanoi high threat area only once per day.
- TOTs be varied to maximum extent possible to prevent a stereotyped operation.
- The size of Commando Club formations be reduced.
- Reconnaissance aircraft be withheld from the high threat area except at times coinciding with strike TOTs.

During December, there were 38 MIG engagements, the highest since May, and 21 encounters and 30 sightings. Most enemy air activity was directed against Air Force aircraft, with 14 Air Force engagements occurring on 19 December. Air Force pilots shot down two MIG-17s and claimed two probables, while losing an F-105 and two F-4Ds. During 1967, the Air Force destroyed 70 enemy aircraft in the air, while losing 21 aircraft to enemy pilots, for a kill ratio of 3.3:1. The Navy lost six aircraft and downed 17 for a ratio of 2.8:1.[36]

Degradation Plan

A joint CINCPACAF/CINCPACFLT plan for strikes against selected elements of the North Vietnamese air defense system was submitted to CINCPAC in late December. As a result of the enemy's ability to coordinate EW/GCI aircraft control and SA-2 firing, friendly operations had suffered high loss rates. To degrade the air defense environment in selected areas of North Vietnam, it would be necessary to reduce the SA-2 order of battle, the command/control facilities, and selected EW sites with associated GCI capability.[37]

The North Vietnamese defense system consisted of five distinct subsystems: the SA-2 system, MIG interceptor system, AAA, EW/GCI, and filter centers. The plan concerned itself with nullification of all the subsystems (with the exception of the AAA, which was considered a separate problem). Since the enemy could continue to exact substantial losses on friendly forces with very few elements of the EW/GCI and SA-2 systems remaining, it was mandatory that every effort be made to nullify each of the two separate systems. The EW/GCI and SA-2 systems should be struck concurrently to reduce losses. Known sites of filter centers should be destroyed as early in the campaign as possible, and others attacked as soon as their locations become known.[38]

The first phase of the operation would be directed against the SA-2 system with coordinated attacks by 7AF/TF-77 forces working from the periphery inward as much as possible. In conjunction with this phase, or following as closely as possible thereafter, the second phase of the operations would be initiated with a view toward nullifying the EW/GCI system. Maximum use would be made of TALOS/Standard arm and precision weapons. The third phase would be designed to maintain the NVN SA-2 and EW/GCI systems in a reduced state of effectiveness. Also, efforts to destroy the filter center system would continue, although the importance of these centers might decrease as other systems were nullified or seriously degraded.[39]

CHAPTER X

AIR FORCE ADVISORY GROUP

Mission

The Air Force Advisory Group (AFGP) continued to perform its mission of advising and assisting the Vietnamese Air Force in achieving a state of combat readiness through application of logistics, engineering, maintenance, communications, planning, air operations, aerospace medicine, and personnel operating procedures. It also acted in an advisory capacity to COMUSMACV and the 7AF Commander on all matters pertaining to effective utilization of airpower, to include tactical cargo and liaison aircraft employed by the VNAF. The secondary mission of the AFGP was to equip, administer, and provide logistics for all USAF assigned or attached units, and to support the operations of other agencies as directed or required.[1]

Organization

To accomplish its assigned mission, the Air Force Advisory Group, MACV, was organized under a command section into staff agencies, directorates, Air Force Advisory Teams (AFATs), and AFAT detachments. During this period, the AFAT teams and detachments were located as follows: AFAT-1, Tan Son Nhut; AFATs 2 and 3, Bien Hoa; AFATs 4 and 6, Nha Trang; AFAT-5, Da Nang; AFAT-7, Binh Thuy, with Detachment 2 of AFAT-6 at Pleiku. Detachment 1, AFAT-6, Ban Me Thuot, was eliminated on 1 October 1967.[2]

Authorized personnel strength for the AFGP, including AFATs and AFAT detachments, was 465, and the assigned strength was 507. There were 195 officers authorized and 215 assigned; 270 airmen were authorized and 292 assigned. The overages reflected in these figures were the result of proposed manpower reductions within the AFGP, based on a revised JTD submitted for JCS approval, and the overlapping of incoming and outgoing personnel.[3]

The VNAF had five wings: four tactical composite wings that basically supported the four Corps commanders and the tactical/transport wing at Tan Son Nhut. The air logistics wing (depot) was located at Bien Hoa AB and the air training center at Nha Trang. The VNAF was also involved in the operation of the in-country aircraft control and warning (AC&W) facilities at Tan Son Nhut, Da Nang, Pleiku, Ban Me Thuot, and Binh Thuy. Under current agreement, 7AF was responsible for operating these facilities, however, VNAF personnel were also assigned.[4]

Since expansion of the VNAF was almost completed, current goals were stabilization, modernization, and professionalization. The Advisory Group placed emphasis on professionalization and stabilization through increased stress on managerial procedures, the establishment of effective command and control, improving the safety program, and further development of instrument and night flying capabilities. In addition, the modernization program was being accomplished through the introduction of improved aircraft, not only in fighters, but also in helicopters and transport areas.[5]

Modernization

The F-5, the first jet-capable aircraft in the VNAF inventory, was assigned to the 522d Fighter Squadron at Bien Hoa AB. The squadron flew 436 sorties in July as compared to 388 in June, the first full month of operationally ready status. In August, the total number of sorties flown increased to 478. The F-5 is an 1,000-mile-per-hour aircraft designed for close ground support, interception, and armed reconnaissance. It carries 6,200 pounds of ordnance, has two 20-mm nose cannons, and operates from a short, semi-prepared field in forward areas. 6/

Additional fighter modernization included the conversion of three A-1 squadrons to A-37 jet aircraft during FY69. One squadron will convert each quarter starting in FY2/69. One C-47 squadron converts to C-119G transports in FY3/68 and one C-47 squadron will convert to AC-47 gunship configuration in FY68. One H-34 squadron converts to UH-1D helicopters in FY69. The major cost of the total investment associated with modernization of VNAF was the basic aircraft. Eighteen F-5s cost 15.8 million as compared with 17.0 million for 54 A-37s, 1.1 million for 16 C-119s, while the 20 UH-1Ds cost 4.8 million. 7/

Considerable difficulty was experienced in the overall programming of helicopters for the VNAF. Thirty-nine UH-34 helicopters, approved by the Secretary of Defense for transfer from Navy resources to the VNAF, arrived in-country in August. VNAF was not due to receive additional H-34s, except those programmed to offset attrition, before the VNAF converted to UH-1D models. The UH-1D program also suffered limitations since UH-1D deliveries could not be effected until 18-21 months after funding; thus, only nine aircraft could be expected prior to third quarter, FY69. In August, the AFGP advised CINCPAC that the VNAF helicopter inventory remained 16 aircraft below the authorized 105, and recommended that either additional H-34 helicopters be procured to bring VNAF inventory to that authorized or that the delivery schedule of the UH-1D helicopters be stepped up. [8/]

COMUSMACV was particularly concerned about the critical shortage of troop-carrier helicopters, which hampered the support given by the VNAF 219th Helicopter Squadron to unconventional warfare activities. The USAF Chief of Staff had approved an increase in authorizations for the 219th Helicopter Squadron from 18 to 25 CH-34 helicopters. For a short time, the squadron possessed 17 helicopters as of July, seven of which were normally operationally ready. COMUSMACV recommended to the Chief, Joint General Staff, that immediate action be taken to provide the 219th Helicopter Squadron with a full complement of 25 CH-34 helicopters and associated pilots, crews, and maintenance personnel. [9/]

At the end of September, COMUSMACV again recommended that action be taken to provide the squadron with its authorized strength through the realignment of available VNAF helicopter resources. He pointed out that the unit was currently assigned 16 CH-34 helicopters, of which 15 were on hand. This left a deficit of nine helicopters below authorized strength. A review of the remaining VNAF helicopter squadrons revealed that they averaged only 1.75 helicopters below authorized strength. COMUSMACV stated that this inequitable distribution of helicopter assets seriously degraded the troop lift capability required to effectively support the important unconventional warfare mission. [10/]

Flying Safety

Flying safety was another major problem confronting the VNAF. As of August, aircraft losses to pilot error exceeded combat losses. The rate had

115

been reduced to 23/100,000 flying hours when a sharp increase in accidents during August focused renewed attention on the problem. The extremely high August rate was reversed in September, but it soared again in November, as illustrated by the following statistics: 11/

	Acft Dest*	Major/Minor Dam	Fatalities**
JULY	6	12	13
AUGUST	7	6	4
SEPTEMBER	-	4	-
OCTOBER	3	9	1
NOVEMBER	9	10	7
DECEMBER	3	12	1
TOTALS	28	53	26

Civic Action

In the area of Civic Action, the AFGP stated that, with certain notable exceptions, VNAF participation was limited. In view of their reluctance or indifference to participating in joint USAF/VNAF projects, U.S. personnel had been advised to provide support only to the extent that VNAF would match that effort with manpower. 12/

Evaluation

In a briefing to the Senate Armed Services Preparedness Investigating Subcommittee on 29 October 1967, Brig. Gen. Donovan Smith, Chief, AFGP, made

---

* Nine aircraft were combat losses.

** Thirteen fatalities were combat losses.

the following comments about VNAF: [13]

> "My observation is that the VNAF is that the VNAF wants to be used. They like nothing better than to be given more difficult missions to do; however, they have not earned the confidence of ARVN and U.S. troops yet, enough to really allow them to go on a day-to-day basis. For example, showing up on targets, split second timing, most of them do, but they don't do it all the time, and they have got to do it all the time, in order to get a true professional status. One wing down in IV Corps can do a good job. Some of the other wings aren't as far progressed....They also are a little bit shy in their night flying. At present, they have a very low instrument capability, just about basically self-survival...."

General Smith pointed out that an intensive and continuous instrument training program was underway. While he did not think it would be necessary to give the VNAF sophisticated all-weather flying gear, he believed they should be able to fly airplanes in most weather conditions. [14]

General Smith noted that the VNAF had some very capable leaders and very experienced combat pilots, but these were in the minority. He characterized the VNAF as "a slightly above average Air Force for the experience they have had and with the type of equipment they possess". [15]

CHAPTER XI

SUMMARY OF MISSION AND RESOURCES

Mission

The basic mission of Seventh Air Force did not change between 1 July and 31 December and airpower continued to play a vital role in achieving U.S. objectives in Vietnam. CINCPAC profiled 1967 goals which involved three independent undertakings as follows:[1]

- Take the war to the enemy in the north by unremitting, but selective, application of U.S. air and naval power.

- Expand offensive military operations in South Vietnam to seek and destroy Communist forces and infrastructure.

- Extend secure areas of South Vietnam by civil-military operations and provide assistance to the GVN in building an independent and viable non-Communist society.

As the air component for the U.S. Military Assistance Command, Vietnam, 7AF continued to advise COMUSMACV on all matters pertaining to the effective employment of tactical air support in the Republic of Vietnam. The assigned and attached forces were maintained at a degree of combat readiness that would insure the success of directed military operations. 7AF also continued its responsibility for assisting, training, and augmenting the Vietnamese Air Force.[2]

The air war had become more intense, as was shown by the number of sorties flown. U.S. tactical fighters flew 62,211 strike sorties in South Vietnam with an expenditure of 91,584 tons of ordnance; while in-country airlift provided by USAF airframes moved 638,989 tons of cargo.[3]

USAF AIRCRAFT UNITS IN SVN

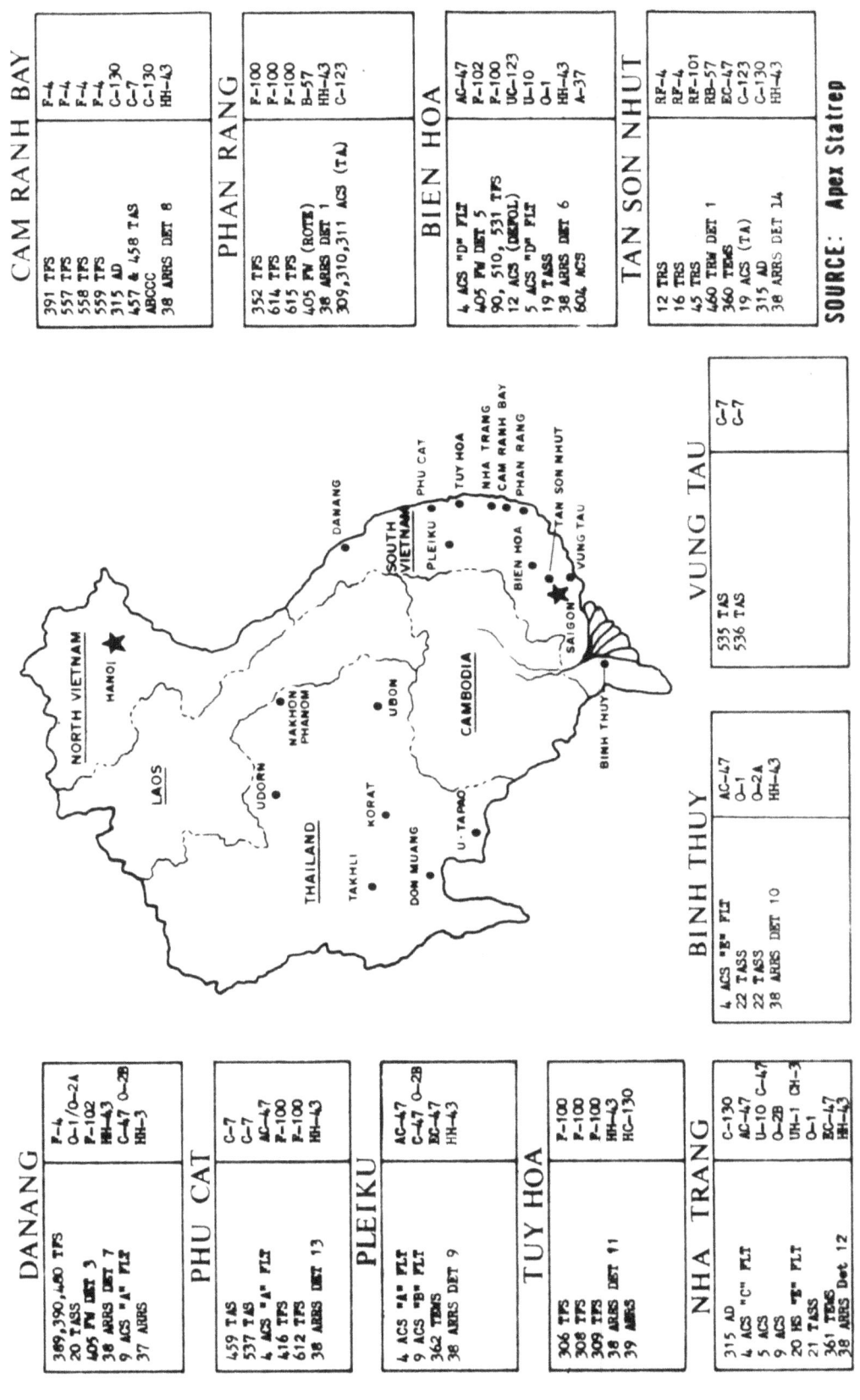

CAM RANH BAY

391 TFS	F-4
557 TFS	F-4
558 TFS	F-4
559 TFS	F-4
315 AD	C-130
457 & 458 TAS	C-7
ABCCC	C-130
38 ARRS DET 8	HH-43

PHAN RANG

352 TFS	F-100
614 TFS	F-100
615 TFS	F-100
405 FW (ROTE)	B-57
38 ARRS DET 1	HH-43
309,310,311 ACS (TA)	C-123

BIEN HOA

4 ACS "D" FLT	AC-47
405 FW DET 5	F-102
90, 510, 531 TFS	F-100
12 ACS (DEFOL)	UC-123
5 ACS "D" FLT	U-10
19 TASS	O-1
38 ARRS DET 6	HH-43
604 ACS	A-37

TAN SON NHUT

12 TRS	RF-4
16 TRS	RF-4
45 TRS	RF-101
460 TRW DET 1	RB-57
360 TEWS	EC-47
19 ACS (TA)	C-123
315 AD	C-130
38 ARRS DET 14	HH-43

SOURCE: Apex Statrep

VUNG TAU

535 TAS	C-7
536 TAS	C-7

BINH THUY

4 ACS "B" FLT	AC-47
22 TASS	O-1
22 TASS	O-2A
38 ARRS DET 10	HH-43

DANANG

389,390,480 TFS	F-4
20 TASS	O-1/O-2A
405 FW DET 3	F-102
38 ARRS DET 7	HH-43
9 ACS "A" FLT	C-47
37 ARRS	HH-3

PHU CAT

459 TAS	C-7
537 TAS	C-7
4 ACS "A" FLT	AC-47
416 TFS	F-100
612 TFS	F-100
38 ARRS DET 13	HH-43

PLEIKU

	AC-47
9 ACS "B" FLT	C-47
362 TEWS	EC-47
38 ARRS DET 9	HH-43

TUY HOA

306 TFS	F-100
308 TFS	F-100
309 TFS	F-100
38 ARRS DET 11	HH-43
39 ARRS	HC-130

NHA TRANG

315 AD	C-130
4 ACS "C" FLT	AC-47
5 ACS	U-10
9 ACS	O-2B
20 HS "E" FLT	UH-1 CH-3
21 TASS	O-1
361 TEWS	EC-47
38 ARRS Det 12	HH-43

FIGURE 9

Resources

To accomplish its varied missions, Seventh Air Force had command in South Vietnam of the aircraft units depicted in Figure 9. The number of operationally controlled aircraft under Seventh Air Force in July was 1,388, with an authorization of 1,572. There were 617 fighters, 150 reconnaissance, 296 support, 228 airlift, and 97 Special Warfare airframes. This figure rose to 1,645 authorized and 1,572 on board by the year's end.

Deployment

Twenty F-4Ds from the 4th Tactical Fighter Squadron deployed to Ubon, Thailand, closing on 20 July 1967. Personnel and equipment were absorbed by the 435th TFS upon arrival. The F-4Ds replaced the F-104 squadron, which was reassigned to the Puerto Rico Air National Guard. [4/]

A follow-on to the present Spooky AC-47 gunship, a test program called Gunship II, was to provide rapid response fire support to hamlets under attack. The gunship consisted of a C-130A modified to accept four 20-mm Vulcans and four 7.62-mm miniguns, all of which could be fired simultaneously. A secondary use of the system would be interdiction operations against trucks and troop concentrations. The aircraft and an evaluation team arrived in SEA on 21 September for a programmed 90-day evaluation. The evaluation was completed on 8 December; the aircraft returned to CONUS for refurbishment and would be sent to SEA as an operations system. [5/]

In mid-July, the Airborne Battlefield Command and Control Center (ABCCC) deployed from Da Nang AB, Vietnam, to Udorn RTAFB, Thailand. From Udorn, a total of six EC-130 aircraft were performing three 14-hour sorties per day covering a 24-hour period. Udorn was selected as the ABCCC site, because the TACC located there had dedicated communications lines to 7AF as the alternate headquarters. Furthermore, the three orbit areas (increased to four in December) were all located within 30-minutes flight time from Udorn. In September, 7AF requested PACAF to provide five additional ABCCC capsules and aircraft to enable the airborne system to control aircraft throughout its area of responsibility--with the exception of Route Packages V and VI. PACAF approved the proposal and forwarded it to Hq USAF. [6/]

The O-2A aircraft came into the inventory with the 20th TASS at Da Nang and FOBs at Khe Sanh and Dong Ha, between 1 July and 30 September. The 23d TASS at Nakhon Phanom, Thailand, also received O-2A aircraft and was fully augmented by 1 December. As of 31 December, 127 O-2A FAC and 25 O-2B aircraft (Psywar) were in the SEA inventory. [7/]

COMBAT LANCER was a plan to deploy a detachment of six F-111A aircraft to SEA. The F-111A was to provide an improved night and adverse weather radar attack capability. The crew training began at Edwards AFB on 15 June 1967, with a planned operational date in SEA of January 1968, at Takhli AB, Thailand. The F-111A would be employed against priority targets to be struck in adverse weather or night conditions. Utilization projected four sorties per day for a .66 sortie rate. [8/]

Manning

Aircrew manning/readiness was well above the PACAF standard of 90 percent at the end of the year. There were 2,241 crew formed out of an authorized 2,261. Of the formed crews, 96 percent were combat-ready. The monthly average of combat-ready aircrews for the period was steady, remaining more than 96 percent. [9]

F-105 crew manning was a subject of interest during July. Efforts were made to insure that students in F-105 training classes, who were graduated in July, proceeded to SEA with minimum delay en route. It was estimated that a critical shortage would still exist after the 31 July arrival of F-105 aircrews. PACAF was requested to put emphasis on early port calls for the next two F-105 classes. If these crews could be accelerated, it appeared that SEA manning could be maintained at 90 percent or better. [10]

A potential problem in F-100 manning was expected to develop by the year's end. This was caused by an F-100 wing moving in-country during September 1966, and the subsequent rotational hump of F-100 aircrews. [11]

The C-7A units experienced a severe manning problem during the last quarter of CY 1967, due to personnel rotating prior to the arrival of replacements. Several measures were taken to alleviate this problem. Personnel were airlifted from the CONUS training centers direct to their SEA destinations; jungle survival school was waived for inbound personnel; crews were retained until the end of their DEROS month; and port calls were accelerated for crews to be graduated from training held from November 1967 until January 1968. [12]

At the beginning of this period, the USAF had exceeded its authorized strength in Vietnam with a total of 45,365 assigned against a ceiling of 44,864. Of these, 5,403 were officers and 39,962 were airmen. At year's end, 7AF personnel strength was within limits reflecting 44,952 authorized and 44,938 on board. Of these, 5,229 were officers and 39,709 were airmen.[13]

Casualties were generally lower in the second half of 1967, with a six-month total of 472. Hostile action caused 411 casualties with 76 killed and 136 missing. Status of aircrew members involved in aircraft losses from 1 January 1962 to 31 December 1967 were as follows:

STATUS	HOSTILE LOSS	OPERATIONAL LOSS	TOTAL
Rescued	445	360	805
Killed	297	190	487
Missing	420	1	421
Captured	100	-	100
Total	1,262	551	1,813

Civilian strength showed a gradual increase in local nationals employed, rising to 12,059, an increase of 1,707 over the July figures. U.S. civilian strength was constant with 51 assigned on 31 December.

The VNAF was authorized 16,437 personnel by the end of the calendar year and were slightly overstrength with 16,767 on board. Of this figure, 2,159 were officers, 14,094 airmen, and 514 civilians. The killed and missing in action were 55, with desertions averaging in the low twenties per month, and totaling 130 for the year.[14]

Aircraft Losses

A total of 232 USAF aircraft were lost in the last half of 1967, due to hostile and operational causes. The VNAF lost a total of 39 airframes, only nine of which were combat losses. A month-by-month description of USAF losses follows: [15]

JULY	-	Thirty-four aircraft were classified combat losses--16 over NVN, 3 over Laos, and 15 in SVN.
AUGUST	-	Aircraft losses totaled 48, the highest monthly total to date in the SEA conflict. Of this figure, 41 were combat, 7 operational; 23 were downed in NVN, 4 in Laos; and 14 in SVN.
SEPTEMBER	-	The lowest number of losses occurred since February 1967; of 17 USAF aircraft losses, 7 were combat, 10 operational. Eleven aircraft were lost in NVN, 1 in Laos, and 5 in SVN.
OCTOBER	-	Fifty aircraft were lost--a record high. This sharp increase was due to 20 operational losses. Of the 30 combat losses, 21 occurred in NVN, 4 in Laos, and 5 in SVN.
NOVEMBER	-	Forty-three aircraft were lost; 4 were operational. Of the 39 combat losses, 26 were downed in North Vietnam; 4 in Laos; and 9 in SVN.
DECEMBER	-	Thirty aircraft were lost--26 in combat; 4 operational. Of the 26 combat losses, 10 occurred in NVN, 8 in Laos (the highest loss in Laos during July - December 1967), and 8 in SVN.

Munitions

Munitions expenditure and stockage showed a gradual rise during the last half of 1967, with 480,900 general purpose and fire/incendiary bombs being dropped on the enemy. There were also 598,000 missiles and rockets expended. Cluster and fragmentation bombs accounted for 40,100 rounds of ordnance.[16]

In July, the munitions inventory included the M-117 high-drag 750-pound bomb. This weapon sharply improved the strike force capability for delivery under low ceilings. The reduced impact velocity resulted in less penetration before detonation, thereby improving the fragmentation effect.[17]

F-4C aircraft began using the M-1 Fuze Extender in September. The MK-82, 500-pound general purpose bomb, was dropped with the extender and produced excellent results as the blast effect was greatly improved. The use of the extender was particularly valuable in preparing landing zones.[18]

CBU-25, during the summer months, greatly enhanced the confidence of ground commanders in the use of CBU munitions. This ordnance--using the BLU-24 bomblet--was more effective than previous CBU munitions, as it could penetrate dense jungle foliage and had a low dud rate.[19]

The FMU-35 Fuze was introduced to SEA on 2 November. It was widely used by the F-4Cs; however, the fuze was suspected in the loss of two Air Force aircraft. It was restricted from use on 13 December, until quality control corrections were made; it was again in use by the close of 1967.[20]

FOOTNOTES*

CHAPTER I

1. (U) Msg, CINCPAC to CINCPACFLT and CINCPACAF, subj: ROLLING THUNDER, 22 Aug 67

2. Ibid.

3. Ibid.

4. Ibid.

5. Ibid.

6. (SNF) 7AF Command Briefing for Senate Armed Services Preparedness Investigating Subcommittee, 29 Oct 67. (Hereafter cited: 7AF Command Briefing, 29 Oct 67.)

7. Ibid.

8. (S) Msg, CTF-77 to CTG-77, 77 CVA, 27 Jul 67.

9. (S) Msg, 7AF to PACAF, CC, 19 Jul 68.

10. (TSAFEO) Rpt, PACAF Air Operations SEA, Jul 67.

11. (TS) Msg, JCS to CINCPAC, 9 Aug 67.

12. (SNF) 7AF Command Briefing, 29 Oct 67.

13. (TS) Msg, CINCPAC to JCS, 20 Aug 67.

14. (TS) Project CHECO SEA Digest, Mar 67;
    (SNF) 7AF Command Briefing, 29 Oct 67.

15. (TS) Msg, CINCPAC to JCS, 7 Oct 67.

16. (S) Memo for American Ambassador, RVN, "Effectiveness of Rail Interdiction in NVN", 4 Oct 67.

17. (TSAFEO) PACAF Air Operations SEA, Sep 67;
    (SAFEO) Special CHECO Rpt, DOTEC, PACAF, "Operation NEUTRALIZE", 5 Jan 68.

18. (SNF) 7AF Command Briefing, 29 Oct 67;
    (S) Msg, CINCPAC to JCS, 11 Oct 67.

19. (TS) Msg, CINCPAC to JCS, 11 Oct 67.

* All extracted portions of TOP SECRET documents are classified no higher than SECRET.

20.   Ibid.

21.   Ibid.

22. (TSAFEO) Rpt, PACAF Air Operations SEA, Oct 67.

23. (S)   Ltr, Comdr, Hq 388 TFW to Comdr, 7AF, 11 Oct 67;
    (S)   Ltr, Comdr, 7AF to 388 TFW, 12 Oct 67.

24. (TS) Msg, 7AF to CINCPACAF, 18 Sep 67.

25.   Ibid.

26.   Ibid.

27.   Ibid.

28.   Ibid.

29.   Ibid.

30. (TS) Msg, CINCPAC to JCS, 25 Sep 67.

31.   Ibid.

32.   Ibid.

33. (TSAFEO) Rpt, PACAF Air Operations SEA, Nov 67.

34. (TSAFEO) Rpt, PACAF Air Operations SEA, Dec 67.

35. (TS) Msg, 7AF to CINCPACAF, 6 Nov 67;
    (TS) Msg, CINCPACAF to 7AF, 31 Oct 67.

36. (TS) Msg, COMUSMACV to Comdr, 7AF; CG, USARV; 11 Dec 67.

37. (TS) Msg, 7AF to 8 TFW, 355 TFW, etc., 2 Dec 67.

CHAPTER II

1. (TSAFEO) Rpt, Hq PACAF, Summary of Air Operations, SEA, Jul-Dec 67;
   (SNF) Special CHECO Rpt, DOTEC, PACAF, "Air Operations in the Delta", 8 Dec 67.

2. Ibid.

3. (SNF) Rpt, 7AF, Command Status, Dec 67.

4. (SNF) Weekly Air Intelligence Summary (WAIS), 7AF 18 Nov 67.

5. (S) History Rpt, 3 TFW, Supporting Documents, Vol II, 1 Oct-31 Dec 67.

6. Ibid.

7. (C) Special CHECO Study, DOTEC, PACAF, "VC Offensive in III Corps", 15 May 68;
   (SNF) WAIS, 7AF, 18 Nov 67.

8. Ibid.

9. Ibid.

10. Ibid.

11. Ibid.

12. Ibid.

13. Ibid.

14. Ibid.

15. Ibid.

16. (C) Special CHECO Study, DOTEC, PACAF, "The Battle for Dak To", 20 Apr 68;
    (SNF) WAIS, 7AF, 25 Nov 67.

17. Ibid.

18. Ibid.

19. Ibid.

20. Ibid.

21. Ibid.

22.		<u>Ibid.</u>
23.		<u>Ibid.</u>
24.		<u>Ibid.</u>
25.		<u>Ibid.</u>
26.	(SNF)	WAIS, 7AF, 12 Aug 67.
27.		<u>Ibid.</u>
28.	(SNF)	WAIS, 7AF, 19 Aug 67.
29.	(SNF)	WAIS, 7AF, 26 Aug 67.
30.		<u>Ibid.</u>

CHAPTER III

1.	(TS) (S)	Rpt, Hq PACAF, Summary - Air Operations in SEA, Jul 67; Rpt, Hq 7AF, Command Status, Jan 68.
2.	(S) (TS) (S)	Interview with Lt Col William G. Podoll and Capt Wesley C. DeLoach, 460 TRW, by CHECO Personnel, 4 Jul 68. (Hereafter cited: Interview with Lt Col Podoll and Capt DeLoach.); Rpts, Hq PACAF, Summaries - Air Operations in SEA, Jul-Dec 67. (Extracted portions are SECRET.) Interview with Capt Reginald M. Cilvik, 7AF, DOE, 5 Jul 67.
3.	(S) (TS)	Interview with Lt Col Podoll and Capt DeLoach; Rpts, Hq PACAF, Summaries - Air Operations in SEA, Jul-Dec 67.
4.		<u>Ibid.</u>
5.	(TS) (S)	Rpt, Hq PACAF, Summaries - Air Operations in SEA, Jul-Dec 67; Interview with Maj James G. Waugh and Capt John R. Tesch, Hq 7AF, DOCRO, 5 Jul 68.
6.	(C)	Briefing Rpt, Maj Charles J. Doryland, TRS, "RF-4C Night Operations", undated.
7.	(S) (S)	Rpt, Hq 7AF, DOE, Historical Data Record, Oct-Dec 67; Interview with Capt DeLoach.
8.	(TS) (S)	Rpt, Hq PACAF, Summary of Air Operations in SEA, Dec 67; Rpt, 7AF DIOD, Defense Analysis Monthly Evaluation Summary, 31 Dec 67.

9.   Ibid.

10. (TS)   Ibid.
    Rpt, Hq PACAF, Summary of Air Operations in SEA, Dec 67.

11.   Ibid.

12.   Ibid.

13.   Ibid.

14. (C)   Interviews with Personnel, 12 RITS, TSN, RVN, 8 Jul 68.

CHAPTER IV

1. (TSNF)   CHECO Special Report, "ARC LIGHT", 1965-1966; 15 Sep 67.

2. (TSAFEO)   PACAF Summary of Air Opns, SEA, Jul-Dec 1967.

3. (SNF)   7AF WAIS, 25 Nov 67.

4.   Ibid.

5. (C)   CHECO Special Report, "The Battle for Dak To", 20 Apr 68.

6. (SAFEO)   CHECO Special Report, "Operation NEUTRALIZE", 5 Jan 68.

7. (S)   Msg, 7AF to all TIGER HOUND and TALLY HO addressees, 10 Sep 67.

8. (SAFEO)   CHECO Special Report, "Operation NEUTRALIZE", 5 Jan 68.

9. (S)   Ltr, 7AF/DI/DO to MACV/MACCOC, "Operation NEUTRALIZE", undated.

10.   Ibid.

11.   Ibid.

12. (SAFEO)   CHECO Special Report, "Operation NEUTRALIZE", 5 Jan 68.

13. (TSAFEO)   PACAF Summary Air Opns SEA, Jul-Dec 1967.

14. (TS)   Memo, Hq USMACV (MACJ-2) for Secy Def, "ARC LIGHT Restrictions and Thai-Based Fighter Aircraft", 11 Jul 67.

15. (TS)   Msg, CINCPAC to AMEMB, Vientiane, 30 Sep 67;
    (TS)   Msg, COMUSMACV to CINCPAC, 13 Jul 67.

16. (TS)   Msg, COMUSMACV to CINCPAC, 13 Jul 67.

17. (TS)   Memo, Hq USMACV (MACJ-2) for Secy Def, "ARC LIGHT Restrictions and Thai-Based Fighter Aircraft", 11 Jul 67.

18. (TS)   Msg, AMEMB, Vientiane to Secy State, 14 Aug 67.

19. (TS)   Msg, Secy State to AMEMB VIENTIANE, 29 Nov 67;
    (TS)   Msg, AMEMB, VIENTIANE to Secy State, 2 Dec 67.

20. (TS)   Msg, COMUSMACV to CINCPAC, 11 Nov 67.

21.   Ibid.

22.   Ibid.

23. (TS)   Msg, CINCPAC to JCS, 20 Nov 67.

24. (TS)   Msg, JCS to CINCPAC, 17 Oct 67.

25. (TS)   Msg, Secy State to AMEMB, Thailand, 13 Nov 67.

26. (S)   Msg, CSAF to CINCPAC, CINCSAC; 15 Dec 67.

27.   Ibid.

28.   Ibid.

29. (S)   Study, Hq MACV (CICV), "ARC LIGHT Effectiveness, 18 Jun 66-31 Oct 67", 16 Mar 68.

30. (C)   Msg, COMUSMACV to CINCPAC, 10 Oct 67.

31. (TS)   Msg, CG III MAF to COMUSMACV, 9 Nov 67.

32. (SNF) 7AF WAIS, 18 Nov 67.

33.   Ibid.

34. (S)   Study, Hq MACV (CICV), "ARC LIGHT Effectiveness, 18 Jun 66-31 Oct 67", 16 Mar 68.

35.   Ibid.

CHAPTER V

1. (S) Hist Rpt, 7AF, Jul-Dec 67, pg XIII.

2. (S) Ibid.
   (U) End of Tour Report, Brig Gen William G. Moore, Jr., Comdr, 834AD, Oct 66-Nov 67, pp 26-27. (Hereafter cited: General Moore's End of Tour Report.)

3. (U) General Moore's End of Tour Report, pp 27-28.

4. Ibid, pp 19-20.

5. (S) Hist Rpt, 483TAW, Oct-Dec 67, pg 1.

6. (U) General Moore's End of Tour Report, pg 21.

7. (S) Hist Rpt, 315ACW, Oct-Dec 67, pg 10.

8. (S) Hist Rpt, 7AF, Jul-Dec 67, pg 369.

9. (U) General Moore's End of Tour Report, pg 22.

10. (S) Rpt, 834AD, "Tactical Airlift Performance Accomplishments, SEA", Jan 68, pg B-17.

11. (U) General Moore's End of Tour Report, pg 19.

12. Ibid;
    (S) Rpt, 834AD, "Tactical Airlift Performance Accomplishments, SEA", Jan 68, pg 18.

13. (S) Rpt, 834AD, "Tactical Airlift Performance Accomplishments, SEA", Jan 68, pp A-1, A-2.

14. (C) Rpt, J-38, "Responsiveness Summary", Jul-Dec 67.

15. (S) Hist Rpt, 7AF, Jul-Dec 67, pg 369.

16. (C) Special CHECO Study, "Battle for Dak To", 21 Jun 68, pg 8.

17. (U) General Moore's End of Tour Report, pg 22.

18. Ibid, pg 23.

19. (S) Hist Rpt, 7AF, Jul-Dec 67, pg 182.

20. (U) General Moore's End of Tour Report, pp 47, 48.

CHAPTER VI

1. (S)   Ltr, 7AF to COMUSMACV, "Future Planning of Herbicide Opns", 19 Jul 67;
   (S)   CHECO Rpt, DOTEC, PACAF, "The War in Vietnam-Jan-Jun 67".

2. (C)   Rpt 7AF, TACC Command Correspondence Staff Summary, 18 Sep 67;
   (S)   Ltr, MACV to 7AF Comdr, "Ranch Hand Defoliation Commitment", 26 Aug 67.

3.   Ibid.

4. (S)   Msg, COMUSMACV to CINCPAC, 24 Jul 67.

5.   Ibid.

6. (S)   Msg, 7AF to MACV, 4 Nov 67.

7. (S)   Msg, JCS to CINCPAC, 29 Sep 67;
   (S)   Msg, CINCPACAF to CSAF, 21 Dec 67.

8. (C)   Rpt, 7AF TACC, Current Plans Div, Command Correspondence Staff Summary, 18 Sep 67;
   (S)   Msg, 7AF to COMUSMACV, 18 Nov 67.

9. (S)   Msg, COMUSMACV to 7AF, 7 Dec 67.

10. (S)   Msg, COMUSMACV to CINCPAC, 25 Dec 67.

11.   Ibid.

12. (S)   Study, 834AD, Dir Opns, "834AD Ranch Hand Study, FYs 68-69-70", 12 Aug 67.

13.   Ibid.

14.   Ibid.

15. (S)   Ltr, 7AF, DPLG to 35 TFW, 315 ACW, 27 Nov 67.

16. (S)   Ltr, Chief, AFGP to 7AF, "VNAF Participation in the Herbicide and Aircraft Mosquito Spray Program", 21 Oct 67.

17.   Ibid.

18.   Ibid.

19. (C)   Ltr, ACS, J3, MACV to J-3, Joint General Staff, RVNAF, 1 Oct 63.

20.	(S)	Msg, AMEMB, Saigon, 23 Sep 67.
21.		Ibid.
22.	(C)	Msg, COMUSMACV to CG, II MAF, CG IFFV; CG IIFFV, 1 Dec 67.
23.	(S)	Msg, CINCPAC to JCS, 10 Dec 67.
24.		Ibid.
25.		Ibid.
26.		Ibid.
27.		Ibid.
28.		Ibid.
29.		Ibid.
30.		Ibid.

CHAPTER VII

1.	(S) (S)	Msg, COMUSMACV to 7AF, 21 Oct 67; CHECO Rpt, DOTEC, PACAF, "War in Vietnam-Jan-Jun 67".
2.	(TS) (S)	Msg, CINCPAC to CINCPACFLT, CINCPACAF, COMUSMACV, 20 Sep 67; Study, 7AF/DOOT, "Effectiveness of Psywar Leaflet Delivery Capability", Nov 67.
3.	(S)	Study, 7AF/DOOT, "Effectiveness of Psywar Leaflet Delivery Capability", Nov 67.
4.		Ibid.
5.		Ibid.
6.	(TS)	Ibid.; Historical Rpt, MACV, MACPD, 13 Nov 67.
7.	(S)	Msg, CINCPAC to CINCPACAF, 29 Aug 67.
8.	(S)	Msg, CINCPAC to CINCPACFLT; CINCPACAF; COMUSMACV, 20 Sep 67.
9.		Ibid.
10.		Ibid.

11. (S) Msg, COMUSMACV to 7AF, 21 Oct 67.

12. (S) Study, 7AF/DOOT, "Effectiveness of Psywar Leaflet Delivery Capability", Nov 67.

13. Ibid.

14. Ibid.;
  (S) Msg, 7AF to CINCPACAF, 4 Sep 67.

15. Ibid.

16. Ibid.

17. (TS/LIMDIS) Ltr, MACV (MACJ342), 7 Dec 67.

18. Ibid.

19. Ibid.

20. Ibid.

21. (TS) Msg, PACAF, CC to AFGP, 7AF, 21 Mar 67.

22. Ibid.

23. (TS) Hist Rpt, MACV, MACPD, 13 Nov 67.

CHAPTER VIII

1. (TSAFEO) Rpt, Hq PACAF Summary of Air Opns, SEA; Dec 67;
   (S) CHECO Rpt, "The War in Vietnam-Jan-Jun 67".

2. (C) Ltr, Hq 366 CSG to 7AF, "Combat Operations After Action Report", 2 Aug 67.

3. Ibid.

4. Ibid.

5. Ibid.

6. (S) Msg, MI Corps REA Coordinator to CG I MAW, 10 Aug 67.

7. (C) Ltr, Hq 366 CSG to 7AF, "Combat Operations After Action Report", 15 Sep 67.

8. (C)   Ltr, Hq 366 CSG to 7AF, "Combat Operations After Action Report", 28 Sep 67.

9. (C)   Ltr, Hq 14 CSG to 7AF, "Combat Operations After Action Report", 25 Oct 67.

10. (C)   Ltr, Hq 14 CSG to 7AF, "Combat Operations After Action Report", 9 Dec 67.

11. (C)   Ltr, Hq 3 CSG, "Combat Operations After Action Report", 18 Nov 67.

12. (C)   Ltr, Hq 31 CSG to 7AF, "Combat Operations After Action Report", 25 Sep 67.

13.   Ibid

14. (C)   Ltr, 366 CSG to 7AF, "Combat Operations After Action Report", 2 Aug 67.

15. (C)   Rpt, MACV/J-3, Historical Summary, 22 Aug 67.

16. (CNF)   Study, Lockheed Missiles & Space Co (ARPA), "Observations on Base Defense", Aug 67.

17.   Ibid

18. (C)   Report, MACV, "MACV Base Defense Seminar", 12 Jun 67.

19. (CNF)   Study, Lockheed Missiles & Space Co (ARPA), "Observations on Base Defense", Aug 67;
    (C)   Study, Lockheed Missiles & Space Co under sponsorship of ARPA, "Evolutionary Base Defense", Nov 67.

20. (C)   MACV Report, "MACV Base Defense Seminar", 12 Jun 67.

21.   Ibid

22.   Ibid

23.   Ibid

24. (TS)   Rpt, MACV, Command History, 1967.

CHAPTER IX

1. (SNF)   PACAF SEA Air Operations, Jul-Dec 67.

2. (TSNF/AFEO) PACAF Summary Air Opns, SEA; Dec 67;
   (SNF)   7AF WAIS, 2 Dec 67.

3.   Ibid.

4.   Ibid.

5.   Ibid.

6. (SNF)   PACAF SEA Air Operations, Aug 67.

7. (TSNF/AFEO) PACAF Summary Air Opns, SEA; Jul 67.

8. (SNF)   PACAF SEA Air Operations, Jul 67;
   (SNF)   7AF WAIS, 19 Aug 67.

9. (SNF)   PACAF SEA Air Operations, Aug 67.

10. (TSNF/AFEO) PACAF Summary Air Opns, SEA; Sep 67.

11.   Ibid.

12.   Ibid.

13.   Ibid.

14. (SNF)   7AF WAIS, 25 Nov 67.

15.   Ibid.

16. (S)   7AF Briefing, 29 Oct 67.
    (TSNF/AFEO) Rpt, PACAF Summary Air Opns, SEA; Dec 67.

17.   Ibid.

18. (S)   7AF WAIS, 30 Dec 67.

19.   Ibid.

20. (SNF)   7AF WAIS, 2 Sep 67.

21. (TSNF/AFEO) Rpt, PACAF Summary Air Opns, SEA; Jul 67.

22.   Ibid.

23.		<u>Ibid</u>.
24.		<u>Ibid</u>.
25.		<u>Ibid</u>.
25.		<u>Ibid</u>.
26.		<u>Ibid</u>.
27.		<u>Ibid</u>.
28.		<u>Ibid</u>.
29.		<u>Ibid</u>.
30.	(SNF)	7AF WAIS, 19 Aug 67.
31.	(SNF)	7AF WAIS, 2 Dec 67.
32.	(TSNF/AFEO)	Rpt, PACAF Summary Air Opns, SEA; Sep 67.
33.	(SNF)	7AF WAIS, 14 Oct 67.
34.	(SNF)	Rpt, PACAF Sea Air Operations, Oct 67.
35.	(SNF) (TS)	Rpt, PACAF SEA Air Operations, Nov 67; Msg, PACAF to CINCPAC, 11 Dec 67.
36.	(TSNF/AFEO)	Rpt, PACAF Summary Air Opns, SEA; Dec 67.
37.	(TS)	Msg, CINCPACAF to CINCPAC, 26 Dec 67.
38.		<u>Ibid</u>.
39.		<u>Ibid</u>.

CHAPTER X

1. (C) Rpt, AFGP Historical Summary for August 1967, 25 Sep 67.

2. <u>Ibid</u>.

3. <u>Ibid</u>.

4. <u>Ibid</u>.

5. (S) 7AF Briefing, 29 Oct 67.

6. (S) Rpt, AFGP Historical Summary for July 1967, 23 Aug 67.

7. (S) 7AF Briefing, 29 Oct 67.

8. (C) Rpt, AFGP Historical Summary for August 1967, 25 Sep 67.

9. (S) Ltr, COMUSMACV to Chief, Joint General Staff, RVN, 31 Jul 67.

10. (S) Ltr, COMUSMACV to Chief, Joint General Staff, VNAF, 25 Sep 67.

11. (S) AFGP Historical Summaries for Jul, Sep, Oct, Nov, and Dec 67;
    (C) AFGP Historical Summary for Aug 67.

12. (S) AFGP Historical Summary for July 1967, 23 Aug 67;
    (C) Special CHECO Rpt, DOTEC, PACAF, "USAF Civic Action in RVN", 1 Apr 68.

13. (S) 7AF Briefing, 29 Oct 67.

14. <u>Ibid</u>.

15. <u>Ibid</u>.

CHAPTER XI

1. (S) Rpt, 7AF, "The War in Vietnam, Jan-Jun 1967", 29 Apr 68.

2. <u>Ibid</u>.

3. (SNF) Rpt, 7AF, "Seventh Air Force History", Vol I Narrative, 1 Jul-31 Dec 67. (Hereafter cited: 7AF History.)

4. (S) Rpt, 7AF, "Command Status", Jul 67.

5. (S) Rpt, 7AF, DCS/Plans, "Informal Directorate of Requirements Resume of Gunship II Evaluation", 25 Jul 67.

6. (S) Rpt, "History of DCS/Operations", 1 Oct-31 Dec 67.
7. (SNF) 7AF History.
8. (S) Rpt, "History of DCS/Plans", 1 Jul-30 Sep 67.
9. (S) Rpt, 7AF, "Command Status", Dec 67.
10. (SNF) 7AF History.
11. (S) Msg, 7AF, DPO to CINCPACAF, "F-100 Manning, September 1967".
12. (SNF) 7AF History.
13. (S) Rpt, 7AF, "Command Status", Dec 67.
14. Ibid.
15. (S) Rpt, 7AF, "Command Status", Jul-Dec 67.
16. (S) Rep, 7AF "Command Status", Dec 67.
17. (S) Rpt, "History of DCS/Operations", 1 Oct-31 Dec 67.
18. Ibid.
19. Ibid.
20. Ibid.

APPENDIX I

USAF COMBAT SORTIES – SOUTH VIETNAM

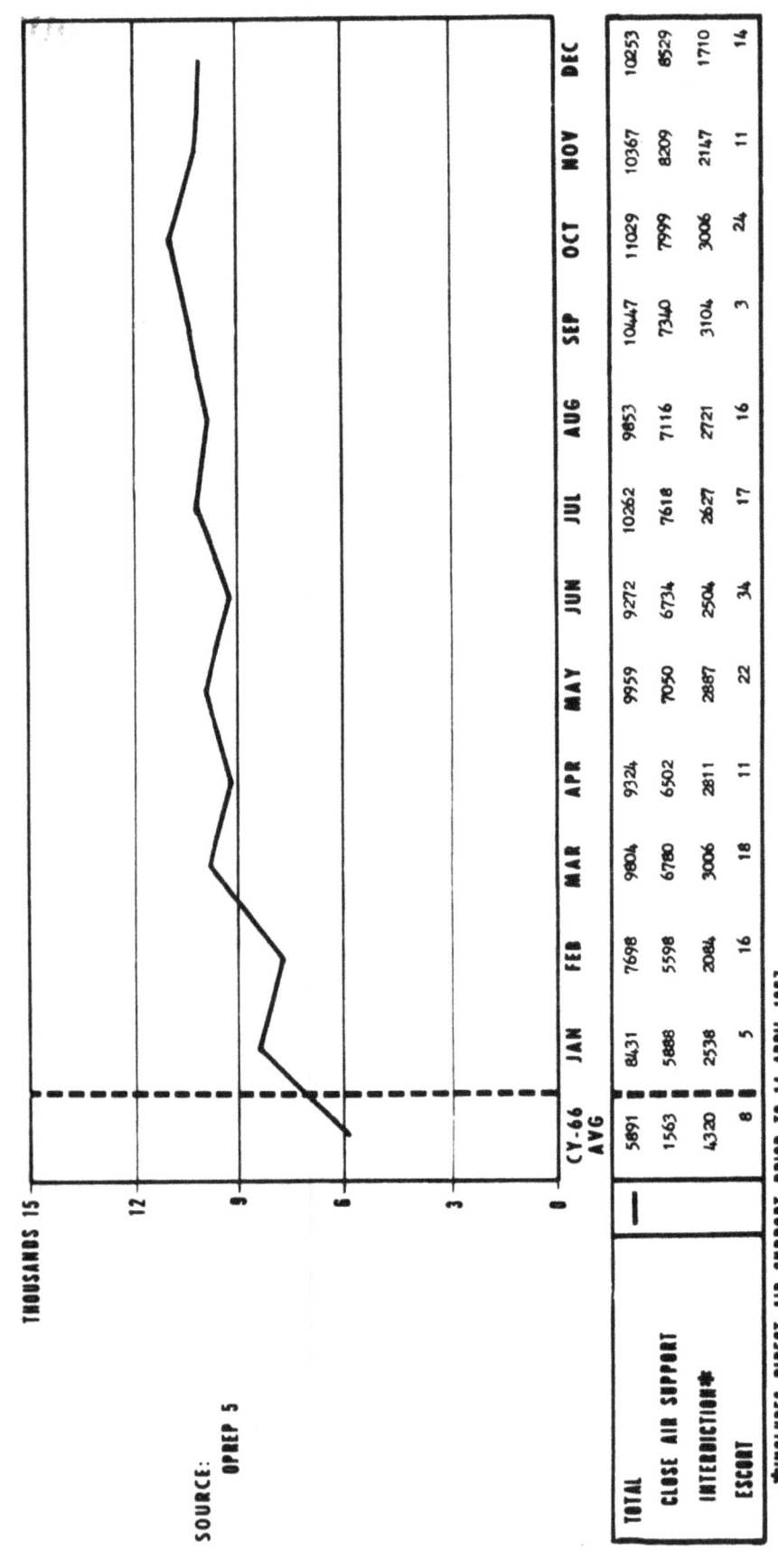

	CY-66 AVG	JAN	FEB	MAR	APR	MAY	JUN	JUL	AUG	SEP	OCT	NOV	DEC
TOTAL	5891	8431	7698	9804	9324	9959	9272	10262	9853	10447	11029	10367	10253
CLOSE AIR SUPPORT	1563	5888	5598	6780	6502	7050	6734	7618	7116	7340	7999	8209	8529
INTERDICTION*	4320	2538	2084	3006	2811	2887	2504	2627	2721	3104	3006	2147	1710
ESCORT	8	5	16	18	11	22	34	17	16	3	24	11	14

*INCLUDES DIRECT AIR SUPPORT PRIOR TO 14 APRIL 1967

SOURCE: OPREP 5

APPENDIX II

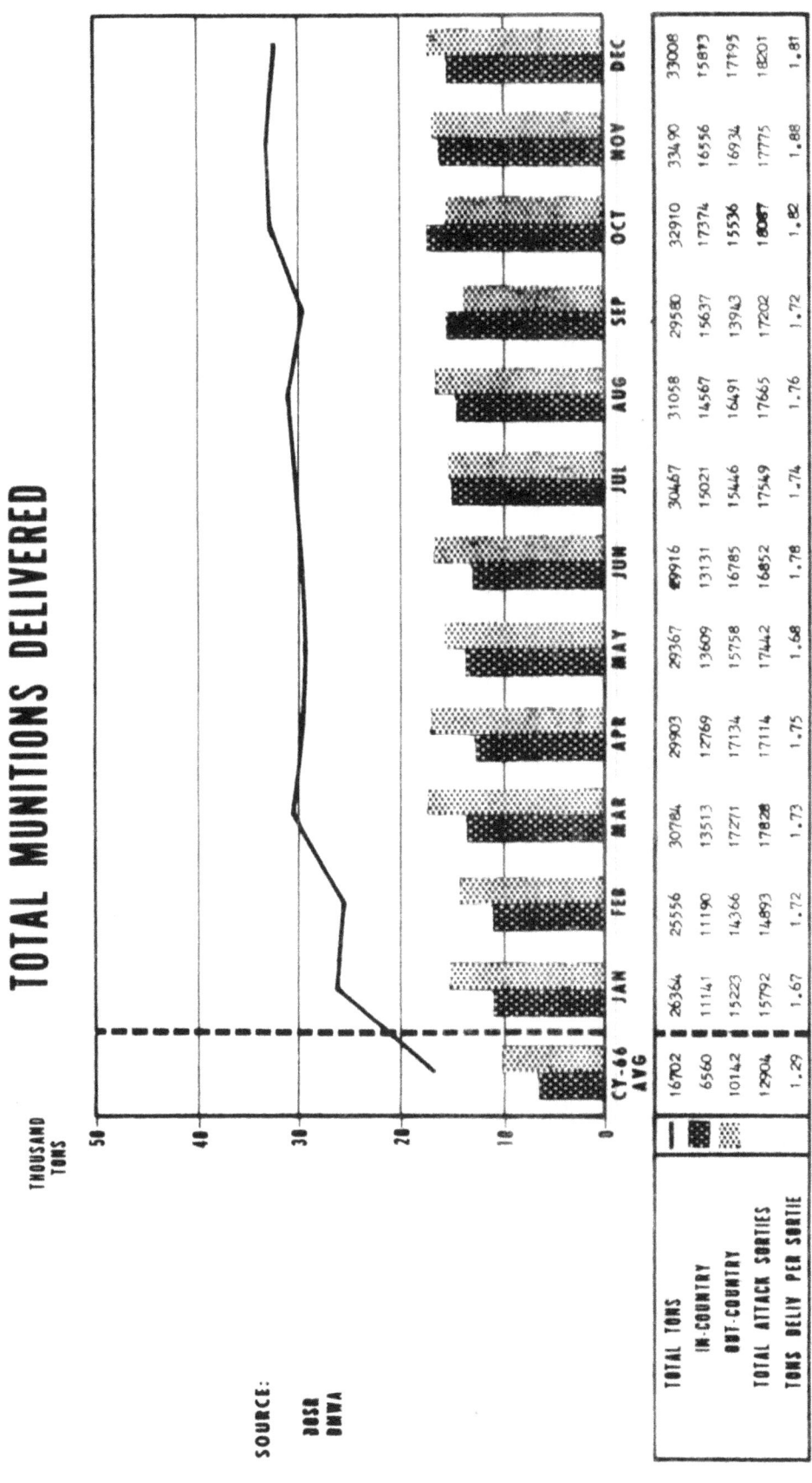

APPENDIX III

DESTRUCTION AND DAMAGE IN-COUNTRY

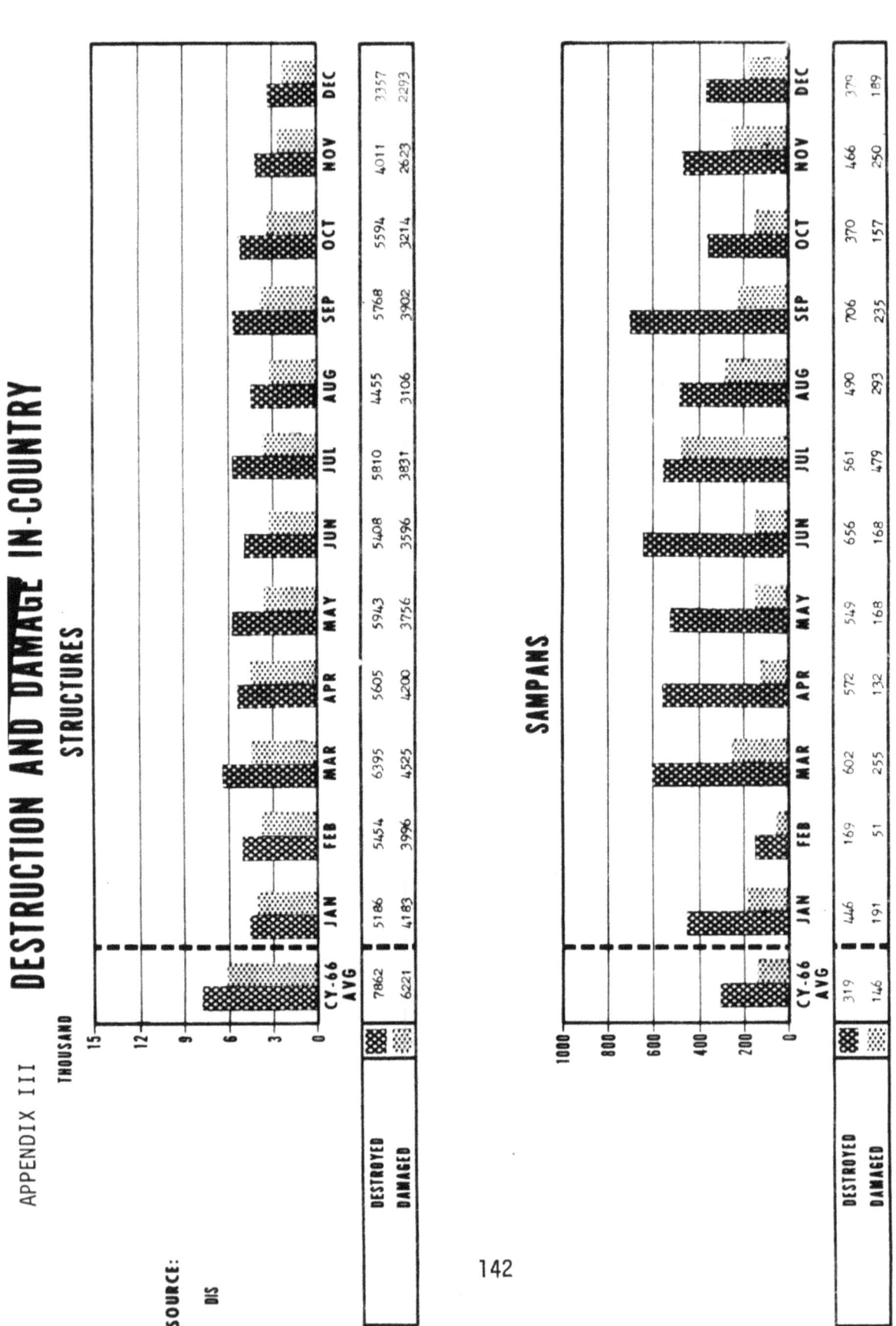

SOURCE: DIS

APPENDIX IV

COMPLETED MAJOR U.S. GROUND OPERATIONS
(3 Battalions or More)

(Includes only those operations completed after 1 August 1967)

OPERATION	BTN DAYS OF OPN	TACTICAL AIR SORTIES FLOWN	TACTICAL AIR TONS MUNS	AIRLIFT C-123/C-130 SORTIES	AIRLIFT TONS CARGO	AIRLIFT NR OF PASS	B-52 SUPPORT SORTIES	B-52 SUPPORT TONS MUNS	RECCE TARGETS
PADDINGTON	63	152	242.0	---	---	---	42	931	6
MALHEUR II	79	1236	1698.5	30	35.5	8	26	568	34
HOOD RIVER	79	202	281.4	21	5.0	764	---	---	---
CORONADO II	53	67	79.8	---	---	---	---	---	---
CORONADO III	17	101	125.8	53	33.0	---	---	---	---
CORONADO VII	2	393	503.1	---	---	---	---	---	14
COCHISE	54	4	7.2	---	---	---	---	---	1
BENTON	87	408	574.0	---	---	---	---	---	---
COOK	81	51	67.9	23	44.0	623	---	---	---
SHENANDOAH II	156	1246	1852.0	126	1329.7	1918	97	2110	14
FRANCIS MARION	1156	3065	6467.0	1	6.1	0	312	6552	105
KING FISHER	200	9	12.4	61	1127.0	2961	176	3872	---
ARDMORE	143	---	---	---	---	---	57	1254	---
KIEN GIANG	27	56	86.3	---	---	---	---	---	---
FAIRFAX	2164	988	1299.4	---	---	---	6	131	118
ATLANTA	79	251	412.0	---	---	---	18	384	17
TOTAL	N/A	8229	13,708.8	315	2580.3	6274	734	15,802	309

SOURCE: 7AF (DOA) OPREP-5 & MACV Weekly Summary

Figures audited and adjusted

* Information on those operations completed prior to 1 August is contained in previous issues of Southeast Asia Summary.

HQS PACAF SUMMARY AIR OPNS SEA, DECEMBER 1967
TOP SECRET NOFORN AF EYES ONLY
(Extract is SECRET)

APPENDIX V

USAF AIRCRAFT LOST IN-COUNTRY

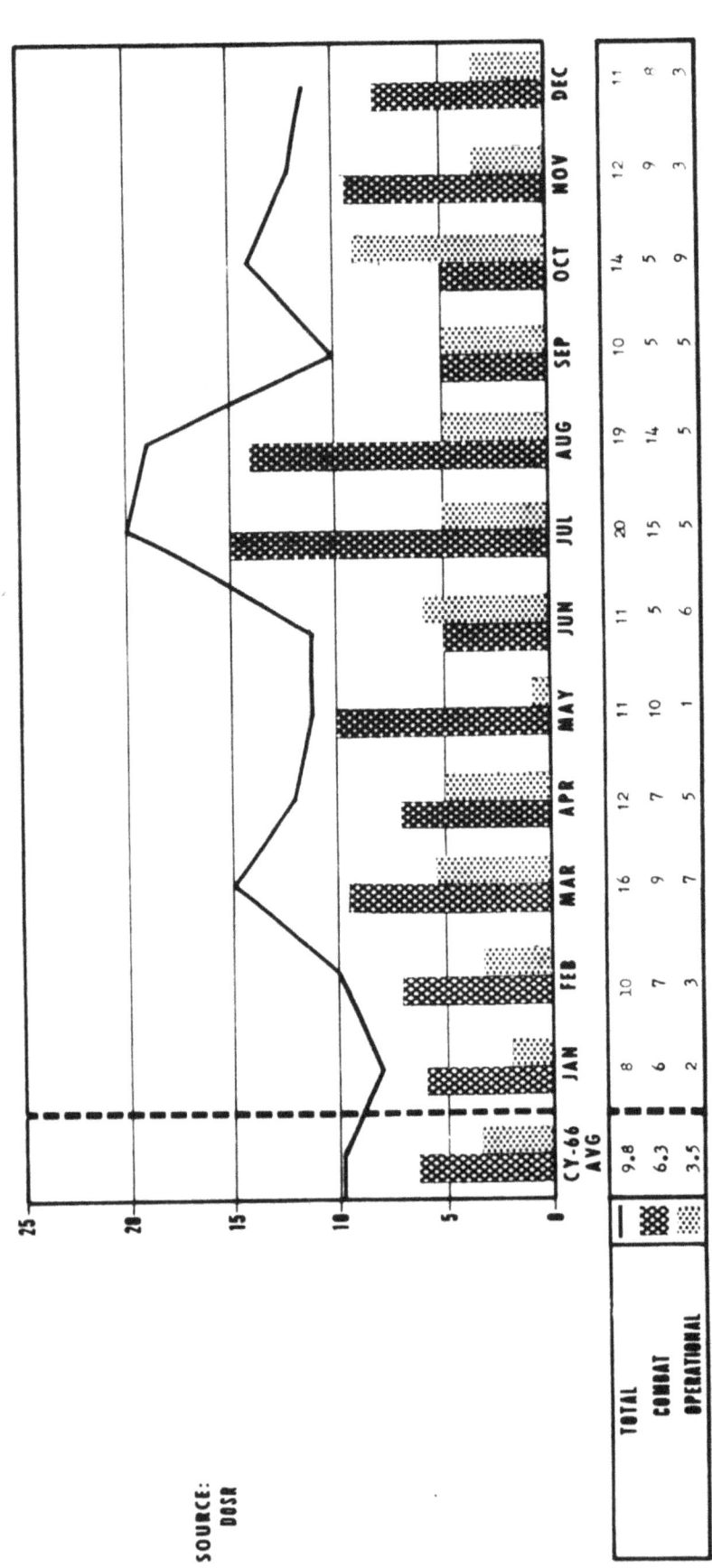

SOURCE: DOSR

APPENDIX VI

B-52 SORTIES/ORDNANCE EXPENDED*

OPERATION	JULY	AUGUST	SEPTEMBER	OCTOBER	NOVEMBER	DECEMBER
ARDMORE (Began 17 Jul-31 Oct)	27/594	57/1254	57/1254	57/1254		
MALHEUR II (8 June-2 Aug)	26/568	26/568				
GREELEY (17 June-11 Oct)	105/2374	163/3650	163/3650	163/3650		
PERSHING (12 Feb-)	45/897	240/5187	249/5383	318/6683	528/11253	537/11449
FRANCIS MARION (6 Apr-12 Oct)	300/6289	306/6421	312/6552	312/6552		
FAIRFAX (Dec 66-15 Dec 67)	6/131	6/131	6/131	6/131	6/131	6/131
PADDINGTON (10 Jul-16 Jul)	42/931					
KING FISHER (16 Jul-31 Oct)		9/198	9/198	176/3872		
BOLLING (19 Sep-)				18/1960	18/1960	18/1960
MACARTHUR (12 Oct-)				15/326	296/6450	376/8195
SHENANDOAH (29 Sep-)				79/1718		
KENTUCKY (1 Nov-)					78/1698	88/1918
ATLANTA (18 Nov-)					18/384	
YELLOWSTONE (8 Dec-)						15/326

* B-52 sorties/tons expended in support of major ground operations (three battalions or larger)--these data are cumulative. Source: (TS/AFEO) PACAF Summary SEA Air Opns Jul-Dec 67. (Extract is SECRET.)

GLOSSARY

AA	Antiaircraft
AAA	Antiaircraft Artillery
ABCCC	Airborne Battlefield Command and Control Center
AC&W	Aircraft Control and Warning
ACS	Air Commando Squadron
ACW	Air Commando Wing
AFAT	Air Force Advisory Team
AFGP	Air Force Advisory Group
ARDF	Airborne Radio Direction Finding
ARVN	Army of Republic of Vietnam
BDA	Bomb Damage Assessment
CHICOM	Chinese Communist
CIDG	Civilian Irregular Defense Group
CINCPAC	Commander in Chief, Pacific Command
CINCPACAF	Commander in Chief, Pacific Air Forces
CINCSAC	Commander in Chief, Strategic Air Command
COC	Combat Operations Center
COMUSMACV	Commander, U.S. Military Assistance Command, Vietnam
CSAF	Chief of Staff, U.S. Air Force
CTZ	Corps Tactical Zone
DASC	Direct Air Support Center
DMZ	Demilitarized Zone
DOD	Department of Defense
ECM	Electronic Countermeasures
ELINT	Electronic Intelligence
EW	Early Warning
FFV	Field Force, Vietnam
FOB	Forward Operating Base
FWMAF	Free World Military Assistance Forces
GCI	Ground-Controlled Intercept
GVN	Government of Vietnam
ICC	International Control Commission
IPIR	Immediate Photo Interpretation Report
JCS	Joint Chiefs of Staff
JGS	Joint General Staff
JTD	Joint Table of Distribution
JUSPAO	Joint U.S. Public Affairs Office

KIA	Killed in Action
km	kilometers
LAPES	Low Altitude Parachute Extraction System
LOC	Line of Communication
LRRP	Long Range Reconnaissance Patrol
MACV	Military Assistance Command, Vietnam
MAF	Marine Amphibious Force
MEA	Minimum En Route Attitude
MHz	Megahertz
mm	millimeter
NVA	North Vietnamese Army
NVN	North Vietnam
OPlan	Operation Plan
OJT	On-the-Job Training
OSD	Office of the Secretary of Defense
PACAF	Pacific Air Forces
PECM	Passive Electronic Countermeasures
PLADS	Parachute Low Altitude Delivery System
POL	Petroleum, Oil, and Lubricants
PPIF	Photo Processing and Interpretation Facility
Psyop	Psychological Operations
Recon	Reconnaissance
RHAW	Radar Homing and Warning
RTAFB	Royal Thai Air Force Base
RTG	Royal Thai Government
RVN	Republic of Vietnam
SAC	Strategic Air Command
SAM	Surface-to-Air Missile
SEA	Southeast Asia
SEAOR	Southeast Asia Operational Requirement
SIOP	Single Integrated Operations Plan
TACC	Tactical Air Control Center
TAOR	Tactical Area of Responsibility
TASS	Tactical Air Support Squadron
TEWS	Tactical Electronic Warfare Squadron
TOT	Time Over Target
TRS	Tactical Reconnaissance Squadron
TRW	Tactical Reconnaissance Wing
TSN	Tan Son Nhut

USARV	United States Army, Vietnam
USMC	United States Marine Corps
USN	United States Navy
VC	Viet Cong
VNAF	Vietnamese Air Force
VR	Visual Reconnaissance

www.ingramcontent.com/pod-product-compliance
Lightning Source LLC
Chambersburg PA
CBHW080546170426
43195CB00016B/2690